Planning and Designing Your College Course

Magna Publications
Madison, Wisconsin

Magna Publications
2718 Dryden Drive
Madison, WI 53704
Magnapubs.com

The articles in this book have been previously published in *The Teaching Professor* newsletter or the *Faculty Focus* blog.

ISBN: 978-0-912150-74-1

Compiled by Jon Crylen

Contents

Foreword......5

Part 1: Creating a Course......7

Creative Course Design (Yes, You Can)!......9
Creating a Course Calendar That Aligns to the Rhythms of the Semester......12
More Content Doesn't Equal More Learning......17
Learning Outcomes for Instructors, Not Just Students......20
Let's Solve the Right Damn Problem: Intentional Teaching with Technology......23
So, What Is the Real Problem?......26
Examining the Role of Empathy in Course Design......29
Librarians Are the Forgotten Course Design Resource......32
Collaborative Course Development......35
Creating a "Build Your Grade" Course......38
Encouraging Engagement by Adding Job-Like Elements to a Course......41
Responsive Planning Improves Teaching and Learning......44
A Game-Day Approach to Hybrid Course Design......49
Designing Online Learning to Spark Intrinsic Motivation......52
Integrate Library Instruction into Your Online Courses......56
Four Copyright Questions to Ask before Posting Material in Your Online Classroom......58
An Engagement Epidemic: Designing an Immersive, Media-Rich Course......62

Part 2: Redesigning a Course......65

Easy Steps to Revitalize Courses......67
Refresh Your Course: Step by Step......69
Keep Calm and Redesign with Perspective......77
Refresh Your Course with Open Educational Resources......80
Course Redesign: A Compelling Example......83
A Checklist for Moving Your Course Online......86

Part 3: Constructing the Syllabus......89

Syllabi: Leveling the Playing Field......91
What Role Does Your Syllabus Play?......97
Tips for Creating a More Inclusive Syllabus......99
What Kind of Syllabus?......103

The Boring Syllabus 105
Classroom Climate and the Syllabus 108
Special Considerations When Drafting an Online Course Syllabus 110
Part 4: Planning Assignments and Assessments 113
Could Your Assignments Use a Tune-Up? 115
Assignments Don't Just Happen 117
Designing Homework That Enhances Learning 121
Teaching the How: Three Ways to Support Failure 123
Reenvisioning Rubrics: A Few Brief Suggestions 128
The Value of Rubrics for Teachers 131
Using Specifications Grading to Deepen Student Thinking 134
Five Types of Quizzes That Deepen Engagement with Course Content 137
Doing More with Formative Assessments 140
Writing Better Multiple-Choice Questions 143
Group Exams and Quizzes: Design Options to Consider 146
From Traditional to Cyber CATS: Different Breeds for Different Needs 153
Formative Assessment Techniques for Online Learning 158
Part 5: Making Your Course Accessible 161
UDL: A Powerful Framework 162
Universal Design in Courses: Beyond Disabilities 165
Culturally Responsive Teaching and UDL 169
Implementing Accessible Course Policies 172
Designing for Accessibility: How to Front-Load Your Course with UDL Principles 175
Creating Accessible Video for the Online Classroom 178
Social Media Use in Online Courses: Accessibility Considerations 181
About the Contributors 184
Additional Resources 195

Foreword

Of the many aspects important to teaching and learning in higher education, course design should be valued more than it is. Many of us began our college careers with a bit of teaching under our belts; we were tutors, TAs in courses, or lab instructors or taught sections of large introductory courses. But almost none of these early teaching experiences involved course design. Most of us first tried our hands at that as brand-new college professors. We borrowed syllabi, copied copiously, and built the course calendar off the table of contents in the textbook. That we were designing learning experiences for students wasn't how most of us thought about course preparation.

Have things changed? Perhaps a bit. Most of us are now on board with course goals and objectives. We understand that putting a course together is much better if we clearly have in mind what students should know and be able to do when it's over. And we do think more carefully and purposefully about activities that engage students, assignments that meet course objectives, and how we assess student learning.

But unless it's a course we haven't taught before or one that's new to the degree program, we're more likely to be doing course planning then curriculum design. The difference between planning and design becomes clear when we tackle putting together a new course. What are the course goals? What content should be used to reach those goals, and what activities and assignments best develop the knowledge and skills required to meet them? How much content will it take to build the necessary knowledge base, and how is that content most effectively delivered? How will students' learning be assessed, and how does the course fit into the departmental and overall college curriculum? Those are the questions we should ask when we plan any course, even ones we've taught for a number of years.

All sorts of books on course design have been published. Faculty haven't read most of them. That raises the question of what kinds of curriculum design materials college teachers might read and use. This book offers an answer. It contains a potpourri of materials that address all sorts of course design issues from planning to assessment. It's a collection of resources from which faculty can pick and choose. Maybe there's a new course to design or one that's been taught a while that benefit from some redesign. Looking at this book's table of contents, you might identify a topic that piques your interest or notice content you didn't previously consider a part of course design. The collection includes articles written by faculty in a range of different disciplines and teaching situations. What they all share is a commitment to those design details that promote learning.

Given how we've been (or haven't been) trained and what we've experienced putting courses together, most of us don't approach course or curriculum design via a highly structured and detailed process. We tend to address design issues in bits and pieces, and this book responds directly to that approach. It's a great book to have nearby every time you work on a course. You can read it for 15 minutes and discover ideas and information directly related to the course you about to design or redesign.

Hats off to the good editorial team at Magna that's once again assembled a great collection of materials for our teaching professor audience.

—Maryellen Weimer

Part
1
Creating a Course

Creative Course Design (Yes, You Can)!

Kenneth L. Alford and Anthony R. Sweat

A lot of teachers don't think of themselves as being particularly creative. Creativity in education doesn't mean coming up with a revolutionary new idea or complete reinvention of something. Creativity means doing something original or unique. A lot of educational creativity involves repackaging or "putting your own spin" on something that somebody else has already used successfully. We believe in adding your own stamp and style to already existing educational approaches—that's being creative. Sometimes all that's required to take a course or lesson from sleepy to exciting is a small but personal creative adaptation. It is almost always easier to modify than to create ex nihilo.

Every program, course, and lesson can be made more effective, efficient, and exciting. What we're suggesting is illustrated by IDEO—a California-based design and consulting firm that specializes in product and process improvement. The design principles they use can readily be applied to educational course design.

Sometimes we lack creativity in education because we work in isolation. Collaboration with colleagues fosters creativity. IDEO, for example, uses a team-based design methodology that consistently results in product designs that no single team member could have created (see here: https://www.youtube.com/watch?v=M66ZU2PCIcM). Here are some of the principles they use when collaborating as a group—repurposed with an emphasis on course design:

- **Encourage wild ideas.** Too often we end up doing what we've always done. We're busy and need to get lesson plans, assessments, and assignments completed in a hurry. But take a moment, consider an ideal teaching situation: What would you do for or with your students to help them succeed and master your course? Let your imagination run loosely. Of course, there are constraints, but letting them go (just temporarily) can help unlock new solutions to old problems. "Blue sky" brainstorming can yield imaginative yet realistic possibilities.

- **Defer judgment.** Whether you're doing individual course design or working as part of a committee, it is easy to criticize new ideas. How often do we tell ourselves and others: "That won't work." "We don't do that here." "We tried that ten years ago, and it didn't work then. It won't work now." "Your students will hate it." It's easy to become "problem spotters" instead of "problem solvers." Early criticism kills the seeds of creative solutions. Like pulling up plants when they are still seedlings, ideas need time and space to take root if they're going to bear fruit.
- **Share everything that you've learned with colleagues.** Sharing insights with others helps clarify and sharpen ideas. There are many times and places to share good ideas and best practices—informal luncheons, at the water cooler, during workshops, via email or text, while working out at the gym—the list is endless. Exactly what you do with colleagues depends on your colleagues and your institution's culture. Don't be insular. There is wisdom in crowds; "we" are always smarter than "me."
- **Stay focused.** Don't try to fix too many things at once. Focus on areas that need the attention or are currently of the most interest. Look for creative solutions rather than try to fix everything at once. We also recommend tackling problems when they occur. Don't let them fester but get focused on different approaches that could be taken.
- **Build on the ideas of others.** You may know the popular song "Hallelujah" by Leonard Cohen. Actually, you probably don't know the original version. Chances are you're familiar with the one Jeff Buckley popularized or you've heard the one in the animated movie *Shrek*. The original song was not particularly popular, but later artists recognized its potential. They built on the original, taking it in slightly different directions and adding their own individual styles. As a result, "Hallelujah" has been recorded hundreds of times by various artists and is a popular hit. (You can listen to a podcast that explains the evolution of the song here: http://revisionisthistory.com/episodes/07-hallelujah.) The same general process can happen in education. Creative teachers often just slightly tweak or alter existing approaches, and over time that results in better courses.

- **Fail often in order to succeed sooner.** Fear is the thief of creativity. Failing is part of learning—for teachers as well as students. Interesting, though, isn't it, how some teachers go to great lengths to avoid introducing anything risky in their courses. In our careers, some of our most meaningful classroom sessions involved something that didn't work quite right the first time we tried it. Fear of trying something new limits options and possibilities. A teaching failure—whether it's an assignment that didn't quite work, exam questions that were misunderstood, or an approach that just didn't connect with students—is not a sign of a bad teacher. It's an opportunity to learn and grow.

Creative course design is within your reach. Don't be put off by the idea. The tasks need not be overwhelming. If you are willing to experiment with these principles and apply them to your courses, don't be surprised when you discover that you, too, are a creative person.

Creating a Course Calendar That Aligns to the Rhythms of the Semester

Lolita Paff

Do you have a system or standard process for prepping a course you've taught before? Where do you start? Early in my career, "one chapter per week" described my course outline. It wasn't an effective system. Poor planning left my students and me burnt out at the end of most terms. For some, planning revolves around syllabus revision, closing loopholes, and adjusting dates. When time's abundant, some teachers read books like Wiggins and McTighe's *Understanding by Design* (2005), a thoughtful, research-based system. I highly recommend their work.

But as I write this article in mid-December, the reality is there are papers and projects to grade, events to attend, holidays to celebrate, and a short break before spring courses commence. Few of us will be able to work through a comprehensive system at this time of year.

What most of us need is a strategic, instructionally sound set of action items to help guide our decision making and provide a framework for our course. My approach focuses on the calendar. This may not sound particularly innovative, especially since many teachers provide a calendar in the syllabus. But I'm not talking about a list of chapters or exams and papers with their due dates. I'm referring to a planning calendar, one that takes into account Duffy and Jones's (1995) rhythms of the semester. Briefly, there are five points I try to address each time I prepare to teach a course:

1. **List.** Identify each class meeting by day of the week and date. Enter calendar items such as holidays and breaks; important registrar deadlines (e.g., drop/add, late drop); any planned teacher absences; and

significant campus events, such as homecoming.

2. **Purpose.** Specify what's supposed to happen and what students will learn: content, student prep work, instructional materials and resources, in-class activities, and follow-up assignment(s). Tentatively set major assessment dates.
3. **Pace.** Designate time periods for the learning, based on content difficulty and importance. Build in "cushions" to minimize the crush that so often occurs. Assume there will be delays.
4. **Chunk.** This can be done around content theme, not just chapters or major assessments. Identify content that should be looped forward/backward to reinforce long-term retention.
5. **View.** Examine the course as a whole. Use special care in planning the periods immediately prior to and after fall and spring breaks.

Creating your course calendar

The calendar provides all the information needed to update the LMS and will save you time. Color-coding provides a visual measure of the flow of assignments throughout the term. Here's an excerpt from an accounting calendar prepared in Excel. This approach adapts easily to Word or any system (even index cards) that allows items to be shifted around easily, incorporates color, and fosters viewing the course as a whole.

FEB 22-24	WED-TO-FRI	DISCUSS INTERNAL CONTROL CASE
		First Post by Wed. 2/22; discussion closes Fri. 2/24
		No class meeting on Thursday, 2/23
28-Feb	Tuesday	READ Chapter 8, page 344-360 & 362-367 ONLY
		WATCH: Asset Cost tutorial
		WATCH: Depreciation Methods tutorial
		WATCH: Sale of Fixed Asset tutorial
		WARM-UP DUE: Problem 8-2A & 8-6A, pages 380-381
2-Mar	Thursday	Finish Chapter 8
		HOMEWORK DUE: Problem 8-5B & 8-6B, pages 371-372
		HOMEWORK: Depreciation Application Questions
March	7 & 9	SPRING BREAK!

Because accounting is sequential, there isn't much opportunity to change the order of content at first. But by mid-semester, I'm able to schedule Chapter 8's easier content before Chapter 7's more conceptually challenging material.

Notice also that we'll be in the middle of a unit before spring break. While many of my colleagues administer tests immediately before break, I schedule the third exam three weeks later. This intentional delay affords students an opportunity to get back into their learning routine. It also allows students to devote more time and attention toward accounting because it's less likely there will be other exams at that time.

14-Mar	Tuesday	READ Chapter 7
		WATCH: Worthless Receivables tutorial
		WATCH: Allowance Method- Aging of A/R tutorial
		WATCH: Allowance Method- Percentage of A/R tutorial
		WATCH: Allowance Method- Percentage of Sales tutorial
		WATCH: Notes Receivable tutorial
		WARMUP: Exercises 7-4, 7-5, 7-6, & 7-7 on page 334
16-Mar	Thursday	Finish Chapter 7
		HOMEWORK DUE: Allowance for DA & Notes Receivable HANDOUTS
21-Mar	Tuesday	READ: Chapter 10, pages 434-447
		WATCH: Debt v Equity tutorial
		READ: Chapter 11
		WATCH: Issue Common Stock tutorial
		WATCH: Preferred Stock tutorial
		WATCH: Recording dividends tutorial
		WATCH: Treasury Stock tutorial
		WARMUP DUE: Problem 11-2A, pages 516-517
		WARMUP DUE: Problem 11-4A, page 517-518
23-Mar	Thursday	Finish Stockholders' Equity
		HOMEWORK: Owner's Equity Questions
28-Mar	Tuesday	Review / Catch Up Day
30-Mar	Thursday	EXAM #3: Chapters 6-8, & 10-11

Sometimes bad weather slows progress, and other times a class needs more time to achieve mastery. After you've taught the course a few times, you can usually anticipate which concepts students will find most difficult, but every cohort is different. That's why review and catch-up days are valuable. Note that some chapters are omitted from the exam and some textbook pages are skipped entirely. Thus, class time is devoted to the most important concepts. Not all content is equally important.

Although not shown here, the planning calendar includes the last date students can add the course and the late-drop deadline. The presence of these dates reminds me to address the needs of students who add the course after the first session. Similarly, students contemplating a late drop need an accurate picture of their current grade in order to make an informed decision. An exam right after late drop is unhelpful for these students.

I strive to have the entire course prepared in the LMS before the first class meeting. Doing so frees up my time and attention to focus on students and their learning as the semester progresses, instead of administrative minutiae.

Avoiding the mad dash

No matter how many times we teach a course, the end of the semester always seems to end in a whirlwind of activity that has teachers and students struggling to keep pace. Too much content, too many projects, and too much pressure to make it to the finish line in one piece.

How did it get so late so soon?
It's night before it's afternoon.
December is here before it's June.
My goodness how the time has flewn.
How did it get so late so soon?

—Dr. Seuss

Careful planning minimizes this stress for the teacher and students. It reduces the chances of "content crush" and panicky "night before it's afternoon" feelings often experienced at the end of the term. Beyond the practical benefits, the planning calendar's greatest strength lies in its holistic view. Using the planning calendar shifts the teaching mindset to consider these rhythms, taking advantage of the highs and mitigating the lows.

Realistically, there may not be time to devote to all five points between terms or for every course. I recommend starting with a basic calendar and important institutional dates. Whenever possible, consider how content cadence or sequence might be adjusted. As you gain experience with the planning calendar, integrating and adapting instruction to the rhythm of your course, the process will evolve into a streamlined practice that reduces course prep time and enhances learning.

Finally, it also helps to keep a running commentary of how things are going as the course unfolds. I call my document simply "Course Notes," and in it I enter brief comments to myself on what's working well and what could be handled differently next time. You'll want to keep the planning calendar and course notes with your teaching materials for easy reference.

To get started on planning your course calendar to the rhythms of the semester, download this checklist: http://bit.ly/2kRP7AS.

References

Duffy, D. K., & Jones, J. W. (1995). *Teaching within the rhythms of the semester.* Jossey-Bass.

Wiggins, G. & McTighe, J. (2005). *Understanding by design* (2nd ed). Association for Supervision and Curriculum Development.

More Content Doesn't Equal More Learning

Nicki Monahan

With access to a world of information as close as our phones, it's easy to feel overwhelmed by all there is to teach. New material continues to emerge in every academic discipline, and teachers feel a tremendous responsibility to not only to stay current themselves but also ensure that their learners are up to date on the most recent findings. Add to this information explosion the passionate desire by faculty members to share their particular areas of expertise, and it's easy to see why content continues to grow like the mythical Hydra of Greek legend. And like Hercules, whose each effort to cut off one of Hydra's nine heads resulted in two more growing in its place, faculty struggle to tame their content monsters.

The two most common strategies for managing course content rarely yield positive results. Cutting back or trimming content leads to agonizing decisions but does not produce substantive changes. Adding content to an already jam-packed syllabus puts us in a race to the course finish line—talking a mile a minute and leaving exhausted students in the dust. Learners in these scenarios liken the experience to trying to drink water from a fire hose. Hoarse, exhausted faculty and drowned, resentful students are not representative of the type of deep and meaningful learning that most of us aspire to.

Perhaps it's time to rethink the role of content in teaching and learning. A fresh perspective on this problem includes thinking about our role as faculty and the role of our students as well as reconsidering the nature of curriculum design.

The role of "content expert" is a familiar and comfortable one for most of us, and the many years spent gaining expertise in a discipline may make us reluctant to relinquish this position. Yet a narrowly defined role as content expert invariably leads to a "content coverage" model of teaching that puts information transmission at the heart of what we do. And while accessing knowledge is essential in learning, it is not the end of learning.

What our students need from us is assistance in navigating the waters in an ocean of information. We can become "content curators" who judiciously select the best "artifacts" for learning, much like the museum curator analyzes and documents all of the materials available before selecting the best representations for any given collection. Our students also need to learn the skills necessary to review and evaluate various sources of information—and be able to differentiate what's relevant, accurate, and reliable and why. If we teach research and critical thinking skills, our learners will develop the capacity to cope with information overload, a problem that is unlikely to disappear in the near future.

A realignment of our role from content expert to content curator also puts content itself into a new perspective. Rather than "covering" content, we use carefully selected content to help students develop the skills of their discipline or their profession. So, for example, students of history learn how to use primary sources to think like historians, or biology students use a scientific approach for testing a hypothesis.

With a shift in focus from covering content to using content, curriculum design also becomes less a matter of determining "what" to teach and more a matter of "how" to facilitate learning. Critical decisions about content still need to be made, but from a different perspective. One approach is to consider the scenario that Maryellen Weimer suggests in her piece "Diversifying the Role Course Content Plays" (2014). Imagine that you meet a student five years after he or she took your course. What would you like to have that student remember from the course? Rather than being able to cite specific facts or information, I think we'd all much rather prefer that our former students remember key concepts, ones that transformed their thinking. Often referred to as "threshold concepts," these critical ideas can become the cornerstones on which we organize our curriculum.

In addition to recognizing the importance of understanding threshold concepts, students might also look back and recognize that it was not knowledge itself that had the greatest impact, but the ability to apply that knowledge. They might remark on the capacity to use a formula to solve a problem or adopt a theoretical model to produce a finished product. If we begin with these demonstrated outcomes when designing our curriculum, then content becomes a vehicle by which we help students apply what they have learned.

This forward-thinking, backward-planning approach to curriculum development that incorporates an understanding of threshold concepts is a vital tool in the battle against content dominance. If we look to the future and carefully consider what we want our students to understand deeply by the time they successfully complete our course, then we can take a backward-design approach to create the learning experiences that will help them achieve that. If we continue to view content as that which needs to be covered rather than the fuel for meaningful learning, then we are destined to fight a losing battle.

References

Meyer, J. H. F., & Land, R. (2003). Threshold concepts and troublesome knowledge: Linkages to ways of thinking and practicing. In C. Rust (Ed.), *Improving student learning: Theory and practice—Ten years on* (pp. 412–424). Oxford Centre for Staff and Learning Development.

Weimer, M. (2014, September 24). Diversifying the role course content plays. *Faculty Focus.* http://info.magnapubs.com/blog/articles/teaching-professor-blog/course-content-can-fulfill-multiple-roles

Learning Outcomes for Instructors, Not Just Students

Joan Flaherty

If you teach, you know about learning outcomes. Unless you inherited your courses from someone else, you've developed lists of them. You've probably had to submit these lists to the administration to be reviewed and possibly revised. You might have been asked to map these outcomes against your department's or institution's broader learning objectives. And you've definitely assessed your students against them. There's a fair bit of work involved with learning outcomes, and justifiably so. They help ensure that we're on the right track in fostering our students' intellectual, emotional, and in some cases spiritual growth. We need them.

But why limit ourselves to student learning outcomes only?

Anyone reading this article probably bases their teaching on learner-centeredness and may even aspire to create a transformative learning environment in their classroom. Both approaches, learner-centered and transformative, require us to shuttle between various roles: the lecturer, who leads students; the facilitator, who guides them; and perhaps most importantly, the collaborator, who learns from and with them. In other words, the teaching and learning principles so many of us embrace call upon us to be learners.

Restricting learning outcomes to students suggests we're turning a deaf ear to that call. It sends an implicit message that our classrooms consist of two groups, each with fixed roles: those who teach and those who learn. It ignores, in other words, a whole legacy of educational thought, from Freire to Palmer to Weimer, that states the contrary: the best teachers have the humility and the courage to acknowledge that they are learners too.

In the spirit of that acknowledgment, I've started developing my own list of instructor learning outcomes. Here's what I've come up with so far:

> By the end of this course, I, the instructor, will be able to
>
> - accept with grace that everything has the potential to evolve into something better, including classes that don't unfold as planned and students who don't seem interested;
> - enjoy developing and delivering each class, even if doing so requires leaning on the adage "fake it until you make it"; and
> - demonstrate regularly to my students and my teaching colleagues genuine enthusiasm for the privilege of being a teacher-learner.

If you're familiar with Eckhart Tolle's (2005) work, you may notice that my list is structured around his three modalities of "awakened doing," a precept that asks us to be in a state of acceptance, enjoyment, or enthusiasm while undertaking any task. That's just my preference. The list could be structured in any number of ways. You might also have noticed that the three outcomes I've identified so far revolve around one theme: meaningful engagement with my classes and my students. Again, that's my preference, suited to my particular learning needs. For example, my years of classroom experience bring many benefits, but they also put me at risk of falling into what Weimer (2012) refers to as "tired teaching." My list addresses that risk. Similarly, the increasing number of international students in my classes brings advantages, but it also challenges my ability to establish a cohesive classroom environment. My first learning outcome alludes to that challenge.

None of these learning outcomes should be confused with statements used in semester-end student evaluation forms. Those statements, such as "The instructor conveyed course content clearly" and "The instructor graded fairly," allow students to assess what the instructor has already done. By contrast, instructor learning outcomes identify what the instructor aims to work on during the course (and perhaps beyond it). Moreover, while student evaluation statements may be modified to a limited extent to fit a given course, largely they are a one-size-fits-all measuring instrument meant to apply to all faculty in a department or at an institution. Instructor learning outcomes, however, are highly personal. They are meant to be developed by the individual, prompting them to reflect on what they need to learn to become a better teacher. They're not meant to be shared with anyone else.

And they're just the start of the process. For example, having identified my three learning outcomes, I now need to figure out how to achieve them and how to assess my progress. But I'm not daunted by the work to come, because the biggest challenge is behind me: acknowledging that I still have much to learn about teaching. A track record of strong student evaluations and an articulate teaching philosophy do not exempt me from ongoing learning, and the title "professor" does not confer automatic status as the all-knowing one in the classroom.

These are humbling admissions that strip away some unspoken beliefs I had been carrying around and deliver me back to the starting place: I am a learner in the classroom. Perhaps my learning outcomes will help me know the value of that place for the first time in my teaching career (with apologies to T. S. Eliot—see here: http://www.columbia.edu/itc/history/winter/w3206/edit/tseliotlittlegidding.html).

References

Tolle, E. (2005). A new earth: Awakening to your life's purpose. Dutton.

Weimer, M. (2012, October 3). When teaching grows tired: A wake-up call for faculty. Faculty Focus. http://info.magnapubs.com/blog/articles/teaching-professor-blog/when-teaching-grows-tired-a-wake-up-call-for-faculty

Let's Solve the Right Damn Problem: Intentional Teaching with Technology

Flower Darby and Wally Nolan

We've all experienced failed learning activities, such as painful class sessions, online disasters, or group projects gone wrong.

When we analyze what went wrong, we usually wring our hands and lament the state of college students today, but is it possible that we ourselves are the inadvertent cause of many of these problems? Could our lack of intentional planning be the issue?

Misalignment in our classes can cause many problems. Consider what happens when the wheels of your vehicle are out of alignment. The tires aren't all pointing in the same direction, making it difficult to steer, causing undue strain and wear, and possibly endangering the safety of those in the car.

The same things can happen when we teach a class that is out of alignment. It's hard to direct the flow of learning; learning activities and assessments become more burdensome than they need to be; and the safety and well-being of those in the car, so to speak, are unnecessarily put at risk.

When we don't carefully align learning activities to course learning objectives, problems develop in our classes.

Misalignment happens in many ways. For example, we might include a group project in our classes with no real sense of the purpose of the project. Have we thought through our teaching and learning goals for the group task? Do those goals support the course learning objectives? Or did we include a group project because our class size grew and we couldn't keep up with grading individual assessments?

When we don't carefully align learning activities to course learning objectives, problems develop in our classes. In our group project example, students will likely recognize that there is no real reason to be doing the group work. This perception leads to frustration and demotivation—not a good way to begin a meaningful collaborative learning task.

We all know that teaching is a messy business and there are pain points in our classes. Our focus here is to investigate how misaligned technology tools often cause more problems than they solve.

It's been said that, with a hammer in your hand, every problem looks like a nail. If the problem truly is a nail, then the hammer is the best solution. But what if the problem is actually a screw? If you apply the hammer to that problem, you're going to do a lot of damage.

Taking the time to accurately diagnose the problem—determining what's really at the bottom of the surface-level pain we experience—is a key step in choosing the best technology tools to solve the right problems in our classes. Instead of dealing with the surface issue, the problem that is readily apparent, we need to dig deeper to get an accurate diagnosis. In other words, we need to solve the right damn problem if we want to truly resolve the pain point.

We can get to the root of the problem by asking a series of "why" questions. Common problems include students who are not attending class or are being unprepared and disengaged when they get there. Let's ask, "Why are my students not coming to class? Why are they so disengaged and unprepared? Are the learning materials and activities relevant? Meaningful? Why am I asking my students to do what I'm asking them to do?"

Asking these questions peels back the layers of our classes to identify the problem at the core. Having torn down the class and accurately diagnosed the real problem, we can now rebuild it, aligning all the major elements to create a structurally sound and meaningful class.

Backward design can help. Wiggins and McTighe (2005) argue that we should plan our classes in a backward fashion. There are three main steps in this design approach:

1. Start with the end of the class—the destination. By the end of the semester, what do you want your students to know and be able to do? Craft measurable course learning objectives accordingly.
2. Design summative and formative assessments that will measure student achievement of those objectives.
3. Plan instructional materials and learning activities to support student success on assessments. What content and practice will equip students to succeed?

Walking through these design steps will result in a well-aligned class where all the components support each other. That alone should minimize teaching and learning problems.

Recall the real problem we identified earlier. With a class that is in alignment, we can now identify technology tools that support the class design and address the right damn problem.

Aligning technology with the course materials and learning activities gives us a better chance of implementing effective tools. Combining this approach with solving the real problem at hand, the core issue, is sure to prevent the kind of misalignment that is caused or made worse by the wrong technology solutions.

When we solve the right problem with the right tool—using a hammer if the problem is a nail or a screwdriver if the problem is a screw—we go a long way toward preventing classes that are out of alignment. In so doing, we create a safer, more pleasant learning journey for all.

Reference

Wiggins, G., & McTighe, J. (2005). *Understanding by design* (2nd ed.). Association for Supervision and Curriculum Development (ASCD).

So, What Is the Real Problem?

Flower Darby and Wally Nolan

In "Let's Solve the Right Damn Problem: Intentional Teaching with Technology," we wrote about using backward course design to align technology with the course materials and learning activities.

How does this design approach play out in today's college classroom? Let's look at "Mary."

Mary is an advertising instructor who is frustrated with the way her large-enrollment introductory class is going. She has several problems that she doesn't know how to solve—problems that we all face in our teaching.

Mary's students frequently ditch her lecture classes. When they do show up, they're neither prepared nor engaged. Another consistent problem is their cheating on multiple-choice exams; the lecture hall seating makes it easy to look at a neighbor's answers.

One day, after weeks of feeling helpless, Mary receives a cold call from a clicker company representative. This classroom response system will solve all her problems! She can take attendance using the device and ask intermittent questions to ensure students are still awake. Also, by interacting more with the material, students should know it better and be less inclined to cheat on the final.

Mary clutches at this solution as if it were a lifesaver thrown to her in the rough seas of teaching today's students. She immediately comes to our teaching and learning center to get trained and set up with clickers for the following semester.

To be fair, classroom response systems can be very effective, but when Mary attends training, we call a time-out. "Sure, clickers are a solution," we say, "but are they the right solution?"

Mary agrees to pause and explore the root cause of the problem. Why are students so bored and disengaged? Why don't they want to come to class? Why aren't they doing their reading? Why are they so easily distracted during the lectures? Why are they so apathetic about the material?

Soon it's clear that Mary herself is bored and disengaged with the class. She admits her lectures are probably dull. They cover the same material as what's in the assigned readings. Mary has inadvertently trained her students to come to class unprepared, knowing they would get the same information without bothering to read.

Mary eventually realizes that the textbook is the source of the problem. It's outdated and boring, and it does nothing to pique the interest of introductory advertising students. Large sections of the book cover dinosaur-age topics like creating effective ads for the yellow pages. There's nothing about marketing products on Spotify or YouTube. There's nothing on creating targeted banner ads or leveraging social media. The content is completely irrelevant to students who are considering careers in advertising.

At last we've identified the real problem. The source of the pain is the outdated textbook. Now we can work through backward design to develop a more aligned, structurally sound class.

This begins with careful thought about the final destination. Upon reflection, Mary identifies her big goal: students should explore whether advertising is the career path (and therefore the major) for them. She redevelops her course learning objectives with this goal in view.

Next, instead of a multiple-choice exam, Mary designs a final project in which students create an ad with a team. This replicates what happens in the industry. Incidentally, this resolves her concern about students' cheating on the final—no final exam, no cheating on it. In this way, Mary develops a solution to an academic integrity issue through an authentic assessment.

The third step in backward design is to plan instructional materials and learning activities to support student success on the assessments in the class. Would reading an irrelevant textbook prepare students to complete a team advertising project successfully? No. Mary cuts several chapters of the textbook, retaining only those that lay out foundational principles of advertising.

Mary replaces the discarded chapters with relevant and timely online articles and blogs. She invites industry leaders to guest lecture in her class through videoconferencing or video recording software. Now her students are hearing from experts who are working in the field and can share their insights and perspectives. Because the speakers and the new content are immediately relevant and much more interesting, many of the initial problems naturally resolve themselves. Students want to be in class, they are motivated to do their homework, and they are actively engaged when they get there.

The result of this process is a well-aligned class, with the wheels all pointing in the same direction: the final destination. In the end, Mary decides against clickers. Clickers would have been a Band-Aid solution that did not address the core issue of the outdated textbook.

Instead, the most effective technology solutions for Mary turn out to be online resources, conferencing and recording applications to bring in guest speakers, and students' own devices and media tools to help them create their advertising projects.

The lesson here is clear. Take the time to accurately define the problem. Step through backward design to develop a structurally sound class in which all the components line up and support each other. Identify technology that supports learning activities, assessments, and course objectives, but make sure it also solves the real problem, the root cause of surface pain. This approach ensures the wheels of your class are aligned so that all students can enjoy their learning journey to the final destination. Safe travels!

Examining the Role of Empathy in Course Design

Nancy Schorschinsky

I believe my capacity for empathy is an essential part of my teaching persona. For that reason, I was more than intrigued by the title of Paul Bloom's book Against Empathy (2016). After reading it, I recognized that a number of his points have merit for teachers. I still believe that, ultimately, teaching requires the ability to "see" and experience things from the student's point of view. However, certain aspects of empathy merit a closer examination when it comes to how we design course materials and in situations that arise with individual students.

We tend to empathize most with those we identify with, and that can affect how we interact with students and influence the decisions we make about course design. So, when student come for help, we tend to sympathize more with those who seems like us. If a student doesn't come from a similar background or hasn't had experiences like ours, we often find it more difficult to relate. It's harder to understand and accept what they report they're experiencing. We also tend to empathize with ourselves when we make course planning decisions. "This is what I had to do when I learned this, so it's what my students should do too." "I hated having to work in groups, so I won't make students do it."

The empathy we feel toward one student may result in directing resources to that student's problem when in fact those resources could be used to help many students. The best principles of course design seek to enable mastery of learning objectives for the greatest number of students possible. When extending help to one student, we should be mindful of the other students who did not come for help but may have similar needs.

Empathy tends to be myopic. It focuses more on short-term needs than on long-term solutions. Are we tempted to take quick and easy design paths that promote temporary learning instead of working out thoughtful strategies, facilitating deeper, long-term learning, and encouraging character development? When assisting a student, do we too often simply address the immediate question without taking the time and effort necessary to help the student gain deeper insights or help them identify potential barriers to their success?

By nature, empathy has an emotional component. The challenge for teachers is to guard against decisions based too heavily on emotional responses. When we do something for a student, when we offer help or make an allowance and the student responds with gratitude, it makes us feel good. At that point we don't want to consider what might have been a more reasoned approach. Are some of our course-design decisions rooted in what we feel will be pleasing and engaging instead of what is appropriately challenging? When a student comes to us with an individual difficulty, do we feel too much for them and ignore the more reasoned options?

Finding the right balance

We can structure the course with easy assignments, be lenient about what we'll accept, and teach in an easygoing, overly friendly style. Alternatively, we can be tough, inflexible, and committed to having students do the work the one and only "right" way, without excuses or exceptions. We need to find the right balance of empathy. The goal is not to fully rely on it or totally discard it but to have an awareness of what empathy accomplishes and what it compromises. Understanding and appreciating that delicate balance allows us to examine our practices in the light of what is best for an individual student and for all students.

Much can be accomplished with a more enlightened application of empathy. Evidence-based knowledge of how learning works enables us to design with the perspective and abilities of all students, acknowledging the complexity of learning methods and an ever-widening range of personal circumstances. Today's students have an increasing array of demands on their time, finances, attention, and cognition. Courses can be designed to incorporate elements that anticipate and appreciate these factors and provide reasonable accommodations. Not only must standards for attendance, grading, late work, and so on be stated, but they should incorporate thoughtful and sometimes creative ways to maintain standards at the same time as they allow for flexibility and choice. Making the effort to plan and incorporate just practices guards against penalizing those who approach course work and learning differently or those who experience problems but do not feel comfortable approaching us about them. The course objectives are of immediate concern, but they need to be kept in perspective. We have larger goals related to what education can accomplish for every student. Those goals transcend individual courses, but they can be advanced by what happens in those individual courses.

I still believe that my ability to empathize—to see things from the learner's perspective—greatly enhances my teaching. Understanding the potential pitfalls has enabled me to utilize that strength in guiding design decisions and student interaction more effectively.

Librarians Are the Forgotten Course Design Resource

Andrew J. Cano

Most institutions provide instructional design teams to support faculty in creating online courses. At my institution, each department has an assigned instructional designer, and most faculty members consider designers to be an indispensable part of the course development process. The same cannot be said for librarians, however, as my experience has been that most instructors view librarians as valuable *sources* of resources but not as actual *resources* themselves. While not intentional, of course, this means that instructors are missing an opportunity to enhance their courses. Similarly, instructional designers, who often work independently of librarians, may not be aware of all the resources available to them when supporting instructors during the process of course design.

All institutions have librarians dedicated to instruction and assigned to departments. In many cases, especially at larger institutions, these librarians hold graduate degrees in the fields to which they are assigned. They also usually possess many years of experience working with faculty from those fields. In addition to their training in developing collections, these librarians bring considerable expertise when selecting resources to be used in class and should always be consulted when choosing textbooks, articles, and other course materials. They often know of material that faculty members are not aware of. They are also up to date on what databases and other electronic resources are currently offered through the library. This is no small detail because licensing agreements and available titles shift regularly as libraries and vendors renegotiate their existing contracts. Consequently, it is best to always include a course's assigned librarian in all stages of course design as the librarian may have more current knowledge regarding available resources than the instructor or instructional designer.

Copyright is another important area for consulting librarians. Many instructors have become accustomed to freely using materials in face-to-face courses on the grounds that this is educational use. While such use is almost always compliant with copyright law, things get messier in online courses because the educational use exemption is intended only for traditional classroom instruction. When making resources available online, instructors must adhere to the TEACH Act of 2002, which puts limits on how copyrighted materials can be used in a classroom. For example, instructors can use only the amount of a copyrighted work that is needed for a lesson, that lesson must be relevant to the course material, and access to the materials must be limited to the amount of time needed for the course. Furthermore, the material cannot be accessible to anyone not enrolled in the course, and reasonable attempts must be made to prevent students from downloading and distributing the material.

Sound complicated? That's because it is. So it's a good thing that librarians are available as resources to provide support in making sure everything used in an online class is compliant with copyright law, including the TEACH Act. Furthermore, librarians have taken a leading role in the promotion of open educational resources (OER) and can often recommend resources that are licensed for use. These include learning objects, test banks, activities, open access journal articles, electronic textbooks, and even entire courses. Selecting such resources does not just help save money for students but can also help you improve your course as, in many cases, they are superior to copyrighted material that is frequently included in courses. This is contrary to a widely held notion that cost correlates with quality, a myth that is probably perpetuated by many publishers. As with copyrighted materials, instructors and instructional designers may not be current on where OER are located, especially for specific concepts. Librarians, however, track these resources as part of their jobs, and some of the larger institutions have even hired librarians specifically assigned to curating OER. Therefore, instructors and instructional designers interested in incorporating OER into courses should seek out their assigned librarian for assistance.

Librarians can help with much more than selecting course materials, though. Pedagogical training is now more common in library schools and professional development. Consequently, librarians can help develop instructional resources for the online classroom, such as tutorials on how to use library-related resources for research projects. It is rare to find an academic library that does not have a librarian who is assigned to online courses and responsible for the development and promotion of such resources. These resources are easily integrated into any LMS and incorporated into the course seamlessly. Better yet, the librarians themselves can be embedded into the course and assist with the development and grading of assignments. Unfortunately, in my experience, instructors tend to be completely unaware of such services. At my institution, for example, we get only a handful of such requests every semester, and almost none of those requests come from instructors teaching online courses. This is unfortunate because instructors tend to agree that their students lack basic information literacy and research skills yet do not realize that they have an excellent resource available to help solve those problems. Consequently, instructors and instructional designers should be discussing how to integrate librarians into the instruction of the course, especially since students are unlikely to seek out librarians outside of the online classroom.

Librarians are a key, and often forgotten, resource for developing online courses. Engaging them right at the beginning of the development process saves faculty members time and improves the educational experience for their students.

Collaborative Course Development

Maryellen Weimer

Collaborative course development is a course design model where "students are asked to play more formative, active roles than in traditional models, with the intent of vesting students in their educational processes" (Aiken et al., 2016, p. 57). The theoretical foundation for the approach rests on ideas of collaboration, empowerment, and choice, all of which have been shown to increase student engagement. The goals of the model are achieved through six specific practices that offer some unique ways to develop shared ownership for the course. Not all can be used with every kind of content, but most can be adapted, and all stand to make experiences in the course unique.

Syllabus building. On the first day of class, students receive a syllabus template that only includes information about the instructor and a list of major headings: Course Objectives, Professor Responsibilities, Student Responsibilities, Assignments, Exams, and Grading System. The final heading reads "My BIG QUESTION (What I really want to know is ________)." Students work on the syllabus template individually first and then in groups in which they try to reach consensus. Then the instructor facilitates a whole-class discussion during which the top grading schemes may be posted, discussed in terms of pros and cons, and then voted on. At the end of the period, all the syllabus templates are collected, and the instructor synthesizes the information, using it to create the course syllabus. Interestingly, the syllabus includes 10 to 15 of the BIG QUESTIONS, which have been integrated into the course schedule. They might be answered during a lecture or scheduled as a weekly discussion topic. This activity could easily be modified so that the syllabus template contains material under some headings but not others. Another option is to list a set of possible assignments or exam formats for students to discuss and then collectively select.

Flextures. These are flexible lectures. "As opposed to topics prescribed and laid out in order, professors in CCD [Collaborative Course Development] courses might regularly (or periodically) enter the class, go to the board and give a list of five or six topics/issues/activities for the day's class" (Aiken et al., 2016, p. 59). There's only time for two or three, so the students decide, thereby setting the agenda for that class session.

This does require more preparation, organization, and flexibility on the part of the professor, so when it's first adopted, it may only occur occasionally. As the materials accumulate, it becomes a more regular feature of the course. The flexibility may be an especially welcome feature for those who've taught the course for a while and would like the challenge of confronting the content differently.

Elective choice assignments. These might be three different case studies that deal with similar issues and require related applications of course content, or they may be three distinct assignments. Students can also be given a choice about the weight of assignments—What counts more or less, the quizzes or the exams? The papers or the final exam? Again, teacher workload is an issue, but implementation here can be gradual as well. The design challenge involved when students are completing different assignments is making sure that each collection of assignments provides the experiences and knowledge needed to realize course objectives.

Creative theory building. This option works better with some kinds of content than others. In the marketing course for which the model was developed, it worked well with students constructing a theory that explained why celebrity endorsements work. In science fields, it could be a hypothesis-generating activity. In either situation, it engages students because it gives them the opportunity to feel as though they're doing the work of the discipline. They're using their knowledge of the field to explain phenomena or to predict results.

Competitive experimentation. Here students compete in groups. In the marketing class, the task was to create the best experimental design to test a marketing issue. Designing experiments would also work in the sciences. In problem-solving classes, it could be problem creation. In writing courses, it could be potential paper outlines. Again, students get involved because it's an authentic assignment. It has meaning and doesn't feel like busy work.

Collaborative assessment. Students contribute potential exam questions or problems. What they propose becomes a course test bank, and some of their questions do end up on the exam.

In a follow-up article, this faculty research team reports the results of an empirical analysis of the model and these six practices. Four undergraduate marketing courses were taught using these six techniques, and they were compared with a group of control courses that used traditionally structured classroom techniques. They hypothesized that the CCD courses would have higher levels of student engagement, higher student satisfaction, higher levels of perceived learning, and higher ratings of the instructor. All four of those hypotheses were confirmed at statistically significant levels. "These findings imply that enhancing collaboration, empowerment and choice can have a significant positive impact on course outcomes" (Aiken et al., 2017, p. 47).

They also predicted that students with high preferences for consistency, the ones who tend to like things to stay the same and resist change, would not be more engaged or satisfied or say they learned more in the CCD course. That hypothesis was not confirmed, nor was one predicting that students with strong senses of independence and individualism would not rate the course more highly on these measures. "CCD processes and procedures appeared to trump preferences for consistency or their needs for individuality" (Aiken et al., 2017, p. 57).

References

Aiken, K. D., Heinze, T. C., Meuter, M. L., & Chapman, K. J. (2016). Innovation through collaborative course development: Theory and practice. *Marketing Education Review, 26*(1), 57–62. https://doi.org/10.1080/10528008.2015.1091679

Aiken, K. D., Heinze, T. C., Meuter, M. L., & Chapman, K. J. (2017). The impact of collaboration, empowerment, and choice: An empirical examination of the collaborative course development method. *Marketing Education Review, 27*(1), 39–50. https://doi.org/10.1080/10528008.2016.1255852

Creating a "Build Your Grade" Course

Sami Lange

Last year, I decided to restructure my Introduction to Information Literacy course with a "build your grade" structure that would provide freedom to choose assignments while ensuring that students learned the core concepts. The results were very positive, and the format can be applied to other courses as well.

Class structure

The class is six weeks long, with each week on a different topic. Students are expected to go through the online "lecture" and other required materials, such as videos and articles, each week. They are also given optional materials to supplement their understanding.

The "build your course" element comes in by allowing students to choose which assignments they will do each week for points toward the grade. I include a wide variety of assignments: multiple-choice and true false quizzes on the syllabus and course vocabulary and concepts, discussion board prompts, research journals, a brainstorm mapping exercise, guided tutorials, summarizing exercises, guided research worksheets, personal assessment quizzes, and infographic creation. Students pick the assignments that they will do to demonstrate understanding. There is also a final exam and final research project.

Below are some examples of these assignments:

1. **Media literacy advertisement quiz (30 points)**

This quiz asks students to find an advertisement and evaluate the advertisement. This assignment builds on readings on bias (unit 4) and media literacy evaluation (unit 5).

2. **Piktochart assignment (30 points)**

This assignment asks students to read one of three provided articles on productivity and pull important content from the article. Students create and submit an infographic with the important content included from the summarized article. This assignment builds on visual literacy readings (unit 5); summarizing content (unit 4); and quoting, paraphrasing, and summarizing (unit 3).

3. **Research journal (15 points)**

This assignment asks students to respond to previous activities earlier in the course, such as the "Are You an Expert?" evaluation of something they believe they are an expert in; how they will be able to use media literacy on a daily basis; the differences between summarizing, paraphrasing, and quoting; and how important it is to evaluate different sources. The journals are focused on individual learning because students are responding to previous work they chose to do in the "Are You an Expert?" quiz (unit 4), summarizing quiz (unit 4), website selection and evaluation discussion board (unit 4), and media literacy readings (unit 5).

Each student can do as many of these assignments as they wish. The final grade is based on a 400-point scale, and there are 510 total points available, so the student needs to choose enough assignments to reach an adequate final grade. Also, students can work ahead on the assignments after the first two weeks of the course as I want them to begin with a set schedule while they are getting used to the structure. But students cannot fall behind.

The student can even skip all of the assignments for a particular week, which raises the obvious question: How do I ensure that students are learning everything I want them to learn? The answer is that each unit builds on previous units. If the student chose not to do the assignments for unit 4, assignments for unit 5 would still require knowledge of unit 4 material. Even if students do neither, they are still required to complete a final research project to get a satisfactory grade, which requires knowledge of all prior material to complete. Thus, knowledge of all course concepts is eventually required to succeed in the course, though the path to demonstrating that knowledge is up to the student.

The findings

Of the 30-plus sections of the course I have taught at this institution and others, this semester was by far the most engaging and creative for myself and my students. I developed the curriculum first and then the assignments, so I was in a focused assignment creation period that allowed me to incorporate many new assignments. I made it clear to students they were expected to learn all the material but could do the assignments they chose, so they entered each assignment with the enthusiasm of having picked that work to complete, and the quality even on scaffolded projects was high. What also surprised me were the students who continued to work after they had received 400 points (which would have been equivalent to a 100 percent grade). Ten of the 30 students in my fall section continued to do assignments and participate in discussion boards beyond the point of already having received an A. The energy in the course was at a high level; students clearly appreciated the options they were given to choose their own course path.

Final observations

One thing I learned is the importance of assigning the right point value to assignments. This can require some trial and error. I will need to reshift my point system on the basis of what I learned so that assignments that are more valuable *and* take more time to complete have higher point values. I originally assigned points according to potential time to complete; however, by weighting some of the earlier assignments as more important, I believe students will be more inclined to complete them. Overall, the experiment of creating a "build your grade" course was highly successful and will be easily refreshed with new assignments and new learning models in future semesters.

Encouraging Engagement by Adding Job-Like Elements to a Course

Hillary Kaplowitz

Making college coursework interesting and relevant is a challenge. Recently, I considered using some sort of gaming strategy to motivate my students, but as I thought about what I really wanted them to gain from my class, it became clear that I needed to do the exact opposite. After all, what students learn in my class is not a game. I teach corporate and instructional media in a cinema-television arts department. I want students to walk away with real-world skills that they can use in their first job interviews and in their lives and careers. So if fun and games weren't the answer, what could I do?

I realized that I wanted my students to take the class seriously, to treat it as a job, and to think of me as their boss. Could I create an environment to accomplish that result? I know other instructors who have used similar approaches, so I decided I would try. I started by using use job-related language in the course. I renamed the syllabus the "employee handbook" and opted to call the whole endeavor *jobification*.

Here is how jobification works in my class. On the first day I ask my students to do a five-minute free write responding to the prompt "Tell me your story." As I collect them, we shake hands and introduce ourselves. I explain that this class will be different because instead of being students, they have just joined a company and today is their new employee orientation. I hold up their papers, thank them for their job applications, and congratulate them on being hired as junior producers at 362 Productions. (My course is CTVA 362.) I show our company logo on a slide and start explaining what they'll be doing in this job.

Over the next 15 weeks, they will be designing a preproduction plan for a client that they bring to the company (course). They will attend trainings (lectures) to learn the skills needed to analyze the client's problem and develop a plan that solves it through media (project). The associated tasks (activities and papers) will need to be completed by the deadlines (due dates), and they will receive feedback and notes for revisions (grades). We will conduct status meetings (class discussions), and they will provide updates (presentations) on their projects. In addition, there will be periodic performance reviews (exams). As their executive producer (instructor), I will provide guidance and feedback on their projects as well as the training and resources they will need.

I review the employee handbook (syllabus), going over those activities that will occur during training sessions at the company headquarters (classroom) and those they will complete on their own time. We go over the job aids (textbook and readings) and discuss the compensation (points) they can earn for their tasks and job performance, including their participation, attendance, and ability to meet deadlines. I pass out nametags, and we start the "new employee orientation" with an engaging meet-and-greet activity.

The job metaphor enables me to stress some of the less tangible skills of business communication and professionalism that are important for students to acquire. I further developed my approach in a faculty learning community for learner-centered course redesign (FLC). In the FLC, we were tasked to consider our dream for our students and look at our objectives and activities to make sure they lined up with that dream. Like many of my colleagues, I discovered that I didn't have objectives connecting to the human dimension, caring, and learning-how-to-learn areas that Dee Fink recommends in his course design materials.

So I created some new objectives along the lines of "Evaluate the quality of their work, interactions, and business style writing as a professional in the context of corporate and instructional media." I used an e-portfolio entry as the activity and assessment for this objective. And for the first time, students reflected about what I really wanted them to learn long term. Comments included the following: "I have learned so many useful and necessary skills that will help me in my career to come"; "I'm glad I chose to take this class, for I have truly learned new skills that I will use in the future"; and "It was a lot of work, but they were experiences that I can use for my career." Others mentioned how their personal development was positively affected: for example, "I appreciated my growth in business professionalism in this class."

Even though I covered the same material in the course, it wasn't until I started using the "skin" of jobification that was I able to help students realize that this course was about more than just content. I so appreciate hearing, "My other classes are based on critical thinking, but this class is critical doing. I learned so much. I can truly say that I have skills that I didn't have entering this class, that I do have now, and it's awesome!" And it is as rewarding for me as it is for them.

Responsive Planning Improves Teaching and Learning

Jane West

Educators concerned with the quality of learning and instruction have called for a greater focus on students' thinking to inform instruction and have offered a variety of pathways for achieving that aim (Brookfield, 2017; Robertson et al., 2015; Simkins & Maier, 2010; Weimer, 2013). These approaches acknowledge the need for teachers to understand students' concepts and misconceptions *as they are being formed* so that learning experiences can be tailored to support students' continued concept and skill development. This kind of targeted teaching requires intentional instructional planning and design that grows out of the actual needs of students.

Responsive planning, the approach I describe here, provides access to students' thinking before the class meets so that the instruction can be designed around their ideas and understandings. The close attention to students' thinking shifts the focus of instruction from what we *think* students know or find confusing to what they *actually* do or don't understand. It allows us to target our time in class to those identified, real-time needs so that our teaching is learner centered rather than teacher or curriculum centered.

What is responsive planning?

Responsive planning refers to the process of capturing students' thinking about course content in advance of a class session and then using that feedback to guide what happens in class.

Responsive planning has the following characteristics:

- The careful design of instruction with learners' thinking in mind, as in Weimer's (2013) description of learner-centered teaching
- The frequent gathering of data from students about their learning, as

in Brookfield's (2017) concept of critically responsive teaching
- Flexible planning based on careful attention to students' thinking, as in the literature on responsive teaching (Hammer et al., 2012; Robertson et al., 2015)
- Elicitation of students' ideas before class and use of those specific ideas to plan what will take place in the next class meeting, as in just-in-time teaching (Simkins & Maier, 2010)

My approach to responsive planning was inspired by Larson et al. (2011b) in a conference presentation on improving the quality of students' reading and discussion of course texts. Over a period of several years, I adapted their work, developing a process to increase the likelihood that students would not only do their reading before class, but would *think* about it, thus raising the quality of discussion in class. An unanticipated outcome of this process has been that I am able to engage in responsive planning and teach in a more learner-centered way. The process has two stages: eliciting students' thinking before class and then using that information to guide the design of learning experiences. Because the assignment pertains to getting students to read the text, I solicit their thinking in written form. Student understanding of content could also be provided by answers to online quiz questions. The process could be adapted for use in online settings as well.

Eliciting students' thinking before class

The course I teach is part of a graduate program leading to initial teacher certification, with the class meeting one evening a week. In the assignment, adapted from Larson et al. (2011a), students read assigned texts and make notes using organizing templates purposefully designed to elicit a variety of ideas and more complex thinking. They submit their notes 24 hours in advance of class; I read them and then use what I learn from the notes to guide my preparation for class. Discussion begins in small groups, where students use their notes as scaffolds, and then we move to whole-class discussion and other learning experiences. I have described the procedures and provided exemplar templates elsewhere (West, 2018).

Consistent with the findings of Larson et al. (2011a), this process has yielded all the intended outcomes: More students come to class prepared, students are reading more carefully, and the quality of discussions has improved notably. The result I had not predicted is that it has changed my teaching. Having access to students' thinking about course content before class allows me to plan experiences that directly build on and challenge students' ideas.

Responsive planning based on students' thinking

Learning to plan in response to students' thinking has helped me shift my focus from explaining what they got wrong on a test or other assessment to helping them refine concepts as they are being formed. Seeing students' early thinking about an assigned text allows me to plan responsively in at least three ways: seeding the discussion with thought-provoking ideas, tailoring lectures, and designing other kinds of experiences that will promote deeper understanding.

- **Seeding the discussion.** As I read students' notes, I am on the lookout for those gems of insight, perceptive questions, points of puzzlement, or even outright misunderstandings that will spark engaging and thought-provoking discussion and move us all toward deeper understanding. When I find one of these nuggets, I insert a brief comment to let the student know that I might mention it when we discuss the reading. I make a note for myself so that, if needed, I can prompt the student to bring up the idea. Additionally, I often take a question or idea posed in a student's reading notes and prepare to display it for all the groups to discuss.
- **Tailoring lectures.** What I learn from students' reading notes allows me to use mini-lectures to clear up a muddy point, correct a misconception, fill a gap, or even to create a little cognitive dissonance and nudge students to question some assumption. Sometimes, however, a challenging idea or point of confusion arises in the notes of enough students that I know the small groups will talk about it without prompting. When this happens, I capitalize on the opportunity for students to learn from each other and instead tailor the lecture to get at other important ideas that the students may not have picked up on as they read.
- **Designing in-class experiences.** The thinking that is evident in students' notes often suggests particular kinds of experiences or activities that would be beneficial. For example, in most class meetings, we view a five-minute video clip of some instructional strategy or dilemma playing out in a real elementary-grade classroom. Based on students' reading notes, I have two or three video clips ready to view, and then, depending on how group discussions go, the students and I select the video that will best meet the needs of the class.

Making responsive planning work

These three elements of responsive planning are all steps I can take in just a few extra minutes after I have read students' notes and don't require extra work. I would be designing activities for class anyway; responsive planning simply allows me to target that design to my students' actual needs. My experience has taught me where students' misconceptions occur most commonly, and I have built a bank of resources and activities that I continually refine and can quickly pull from as needed.

The same responsive planning process can be adapted to a variety of preparatory assignments. What matters is not the particular pre-class assignment but rather how the instructor uses the information about students' thinking. For large classes, the assignment might be an online quiz on the concepts to be taught. Drinkwater et al. (2014) used this strategy in undergraduate physics classes of 200 to 300 students. The students read assigned texts and took a brief online quiz 12 hours before class. A computer analysis provided common themes in student responses, and instructors used those themes to tailor lectures and plan active learning activities.

Several of the classroom assessment techniques developed by Angelo and Cross (1993) could be adapted for use in responsive planning. Using the technique called "muddiest point," for instance, one might simply ask students to identify their greatest areas of confusion and submit them several hours before class. The professor could then use those areas of confusion in the final stages of planning for class, seeding discussion, tailoring lectures, and designing other learning experiences.

Conclusion

According to Weimer (2013), learner-centered teaching is less scripted than more traditional teaching, and this uncertainty sometimes makes us faculty members nervous. Planning responsively from students' pre-class submissions helps to address some of that uncertainty. An instructor with some insight into what students are thinking has the opportunity to reflect on their ideas, assumptions, questions, and misconceptions and to plan for class in ways that best support and challenge those students. Attempting to place students' thinking at the center of our teaching is not new. Responsive planning offers a way to design instruction that is driven not only by the instructor's professional knowledge and experience, but also by real-time data about how particular students are making meaning about course content.

References

Angelo, T. A., & Cross, K. P. (1993). *Classroom assessment techniques: A handbook for college teachers* (2nd ed.). Jossey-Bass.

Brookfield, S. D. (2017). *Becoming a critically reflective teacher* (2nd ed.). Jossey-Bass.

Drinkwater, M. J. Gannaway, D., Sheppard, K., Davis, M. J., Wegener, M. J., Bowen, W. P., & Corney, J. F. (2014). Managing active learning processes in large first year physics classes: The advantages of an integrated approach. *Teaching & Learning Inquiry, 2*(2), 75–90.

Hammer, D., Goldberg, F., & Fargason, S. (2012). Responsive teaching and the beginnings of energy in a third-grade classroom. *Review of Science, Mathematics, and ICT Education, 6*, 51–72.

Larson, J., Young, A. I., & Leipham, M. B. (2011a). Reading to learn: Engaging university students in meaningful reading and discussion. *Teaching Journalism and Mass Communication, 1*(1), 1–11.

Larson, J., Young, A. & Leipham, M. B. (2011b, October). Reading to learn: If students won't read, how can they learn? Paper presented at the Annual Conference of the International Society for the Scholarship of Teaching and Learning (ISSOTL), Milwaukee, WI.

Robertson, A. D., Scherr, R., & Hammer, D. (Eds.). (2015). *Responsive teaching in science and mathematics*. Routledge.

Simkins, S., & Maier, M. (Eds.). (2010). *Just-in-time teaching: Across the disciplines, across the academy*. Stylus Publishing.

Weimer, M. (2013). *Learner-centered teaching: Five key changes to practice* (2nd ed.). Jossey-Bass.

West, J. (2018). Raising the quality of discussion by scaffolding students' reading. *International Journal of Teaching and Learning in Higher Education, 30*(1), 146–160.

A Game-Day Approach to Hybrid Course Design

Bradley Bowers

Students arrive in our courses with a variety strengths and weaknesses. In a writing course, some students may struggle with grammar, while others are ready to practice alternative styles of discourse or more sophisticated rhetorical techniques.

For those students with deficiencies, it can be intimidating working with the better prepared students. Rather than learning from the more advanced students, the experience may reinforce insecurities they have about their own abilities. But that doesn't discount the many benefits of working with peers. It all comes down to the design.

I developed a team model for my hybrid introduction to literature course, and it's an approach that's proven successful. This course is designed to serve a diverse student body, including first-generation students who often lack the preparation to succeed in a course that emphasizes writing and research skills. The team metaphor is ideal because a team is built on mutual support between players toward a common goal. Each player brings their own strengths and weaknesses to the team, and similarly, the online and face-to-face collaboration in this course allows each student to contribute in a particular way to winning the game, based on their role on the team.

Team format

To facilitate a team environment, I modeled the online components as practices and face-to-face sessions as game days. Students work with their team in the online component to develop their assignments, and then during class time they present what they learned. In this way, the team supports each student much like athletic teams support each player.

One of the most successful tools in this hybrid course turned out to be made of paper and plastic: the course notebook. On the first day of class, I put students into groups and gave each student a slender notebook binder with section dividers, paper for notes, and copies of all assignments and handouts. As a team-building exercise, each group assembled the notebooks in class; they chose a group name; they talked about their individual strengths and weaknesses as writers. Finally, based on their self-described individual strengths, they delegated specific writing, editing, and research responsibilities to each member. Each group became a unique team, and the notebooks became the game plan. Students indicated that having a tangible guide with them made the game plan easier to follow.

Each student was responsible for online discussion board postings, contributing to drafts and finished assignments, and responding to the other students' posted drafts and comments. The team captain was responsible for monitoring the discussions. My role was that of a coach—supporting, evaluating, and encouraging—as opposed to the usual characterization of the instructor as the referee. I initiated each discussion board thread with a question and interacted in the ensuing discussion. I also critiqued each draft of each essay that was posted (after each student in the group had submitted a critique).

The teams used the face-to-face class sessions for final editing and oral presentations of final papers, which other students evaluated using a rubric. The competition in this course was "friendly" since the teams were competing against the rubric's requirements, not against each other. Students readily embraced the team approach, and high-risk students found support from others, not judgement.

Four strategies for effective teams

Faculty interested in developing their own courses on a team model need only keep a few best practices in mind:

- **Create an incentive for students to help one another.** In this course, each team received the same final score on a project; however, it was not a "group grade" but the combined total score of each team member; therefore, students were motivated to help each team member achieve their best, since helping individual team members succeed let the whole team succeed.
- **Coach students on teamwork.** The teams who were most successful communicated frequently throughout the course, using primarily email but also the discussion boards to ask questions or receive feedback on drafts and papers. Since students in a group are usually loathe to criticize their peers, in my role as "coach" I asked team

members not to criticize but to give encouragement and possibly offer guidance, but with no requirements as to the email or post's length. Often it was a simple "high-five," but they would also offer ideas on how to improve.

- **Treat the course as a season.** The notebook was an idea that grew from my own need to organize the course well in advance; however, it allowed students to see where the course was going and to locate the exact assignments and handouts for each date and deadline while they worked by themselves online. This allowed them to view the course as a kind of season with assignments as games.
- **Make the face-to-face component important.** Faculty often struggle to come up with interesting activities in the face-to-face component of a hybrid course. In our case, because they were either game days or preparations for game days, students realized that each face-to-face class period was important. The limited time together greatly enhanced the use of that time, forcing the teams to collaborate toward accomplishing the goals of that day.

The peer pressure on each team member on "game day" became apparent around midway through the course, and those teams that were struggling revised their game plans. In the end, all teams received an A or B in the course. About two-thirds of the students were student-athletes, and among the nonathletes, two students were weaker members of their teams and one dropped the course. However, the nonathletes were drawn into the team sport aspect of the course, perhaps because a required course had transformed into preparation for a fierce but friendly game-day competition.

Consider transforming your hybrid courses into a team model to improve the performance of all students.

Designing Online Learning to Spark Intrinsic Motivation

Rebecca Zambrano

The word *motivation* comes from a root that means "to move," and really, motivation is about what moves us to begin something or to persist in a situation—in this case, a learning situation. Motivation is a driving force. It can be considered an external driving force, something that motivates us from the outside, or a psychological force that compels us toward an action or a goal from the inside.

Extrinsic motivation—such as money or job security as motivators—is reward-based. We're moved to do something or persist because we want a reward of some kind that will come from completing the task. Intrinsic motivation is different. Curiosity, love of learning, the ability to use new knowledge and apply it to one's own goals: all of these are things that are intrinsically motivating to people. They're motivating because they're enjoyable or because they satisfy an internal psychological desire.

Studies by Deci and Ryan have shown that intrinsic motivation tends to produce much deeper and more sustained engagement and learning than extrinsic motivation. And these studies have been followed up by many other studies that tend to have similar results.

Deci's 1996 book, *Why We Do What We Do: Understanding Self-Motivation*, includes a theory called self-determination theory, based on three categories of intrinsic motivation that the author claims are universal to all human beings. He argues that these three categories—competence, connection, and autonomy—are actually needs that all of us have to meet in our lives in order to experience our optimal potential as humans.

When all three of these needs are met, according to self-determination theory, we sustain our desire to keep learning. We sustain our desire to produce, to keep producing, to be creative, and to give our time and energy to others and, in general, increase and sustain our desire to live all the roles that we play in our lives to the best of our ability. But when one of these three needs is not met in some area, our motivation may suffer.

So in any learning situation, the student would, ideally, have all three needs met in order to want to sustain that learning over time without the need for the reward of money or grades or some other extrinsic motivator.

Looking at practical applications of the theory, one of the ways to think about this is that each student has a unique motivational profile of underlying desire and drives; as an instructor, getting to know students well can often make obvious what the main motivators are for particular students. Most students want to get a good grade, but it is the intrinsic motivators, such as the need to gain competence in a course or the need to have a sense of choice or a sense of directing their own learning to some degree or another, that motivates students to succeed.

Each student will have a different mix of those needs. It's often true, for example, that when professionals, as opposed to traditional students, come into an online class, their need to connect and network with others in the online format may not be as strong, and their need may be really more about gaining competence.

It is important for instructors to ask questions and reach out to students in order to learn more about their own specific motivational profiles. And, of course, if we were to ask them, "What is your motivational profile?" they probably wouldn't have a clue what to say. But questions about what they most liked or enjoyed about the learning in a particular assignment, what aspect of the assignment they didn't enjoy, or what was challenging for them—the answers to these questions give clues to their particular motivational profiles.

Not only can that help direct the learning in that course, but that feedback can be used in a redesign of a course later on. Before designing or improving an online course, ask some core questions: Why do people want to take the course? What is it that students are coming to class to gain? Are they there to learn skills? Are they there to tap into the creative potential of others who are working to solve complex issues in their workplaces?

Sometimes it's fair to assume that students want connectedness with others, but in a research class in a doctoral program, they may really want mentorship from the instructor of that class and not seek so much interaction with others. So, again, asking these questions can help in designing the most motivating kinds of assignments for the courses that you teach.

It's also true though that even if an instructor has a very good understanding of the particular student population, there will be diversity within each course. So it is important to design with that in mind. Create a mix of assignments that recognizes the diversity of motivational profiles of students in all courses and include a choice of assignments where possible.

Developmental assignments

The idea behind a developmental assignment is that it helps students gain mastery over time at increasing levels of depth. For example, at the beginning of a course, students might be provided with a difficult case scenario that they have very little ability to solve or to analyze, but that they will have an increasing ability to solve or analyze over time. They revisit that same scenario a couple of weeks after the start of the course and write a whole new response or a whole new analysis that includes the learning that they have already done up to that point. Depending on the assignment and the level of complexity, students might revisit that case scenario three times, or it could be every week during the course.

But the key is for students to watch their own learning and ability grow over time. Which of Ryan and Deci's three motivational needs would that apply to? Let's revisit those three needs. One is competence, one is relatedness with others, and one is autonomy or freedom.

This developmental type of assignment meets the need for competence as students are watching their abilities grow over time if they are successful.

In illustrating their abilities, students are also able to meet their need for autonomy. There are also ways to *add* autonomy to an assignment like this. When students have a choice, for example, in how they're going to present their increasing levels of skill, it can help with autonomy.

The developmental assignment can also increase the students' sense of belonging and relatedness. If, for example, they share their final analysis with others in the course, or maybe their halfway-through analysis, or they seek support from others in the course, that could also meet the need for relatedness.

These categories are not always clear-cut, and that's not a bad thing. They're really there to help instructors think about how to increase the level of intrinsic motivation in their assignments.

The key to the developmental assignment is that students are revisiting in greater depth or complexity over time. They're revisiting the same content, to analyze it or discuss it and pull it apart, or maybe to add knowledge over time.

Autonomy

There are many ways to allow students to guide aspects of their learning, and very clearly meeting one of the needs that Ryan and Deci identify: the need for autonomy. One way to do so would be to invite students to create evaluation criteria for an assignment and offer their suggestions for criteria for a rubric. Students very much appreciate being given the chance to determine parts of how they're going to be evaluated.

Giving students a choice about what sections or chapters to cover also provides autonomy, as does allowing them to choose the exam format—for example, multiple choice versus essay.

There is more than one way to help students become free. Freedom can mean giving students more choice of what to do or how to do it inside our classrooms. But freedom can also mean freeing up our perspectives, and one way to do so is to examine multiple perspectives on the same topic.

Recognizing a lack of motivation

Some students do not come into class feeling as if their voices are valuable to the learning community. This can be true for a variety of reasons. In some cases, it may be because the content is so new to them that they don't really feel that they have a lot to add. In other cases, students may come into a course with a language background that isn't standard English or doesn't match the academic English that's being used in the course. I think that can make some students very silent in our class discussion forums, at least initially.

In cases like this, how might an instructor intervene?

One of the clearest indicators of a lack of motivation is a lack of participation. In the online classroom, quality of communication can be quite important. If an instructor only uses the word count feature of the LMS, a lack of motivation can be easily missed, as students can obviously write a lot and not say very much in a discussion forum.

An early indicator is a student missing in action or typing just short little posts that lack much thought. When that happens, it's important to immediately contact the student by email or even phone. This can be a wakeup call, but the idea is definitely not to scare them. It's to have a supportive conversation and to remind the student of the shared goals of the class.

Adapted from the Magna Online Seminar presentation, *Designing Online Learning to Spark Intrinsic Motivation.*

Integrate Library Instruction into Your Online Courses

Andrew J. Cano

Information literacy is critical to the success of a student as many students fail due to not knowing how to find quality resources. While many instructors recognize this need, they normally incorporate it into their courses by asking a librarian to come in to do a library session or tour of the actual library. But as an undergraduate, I took these as days to mentally "check out," and enjoy what I considered to be a break from the "real" learning. Even in my graduate studies, I never appreciated the benefits of what the library could offer me as a student (ironically, since I was studying to be a librarian), precisely because I viewed library instruction as something optional. A far better method is to integrate library instruction into the course itself. Fortunately, online classrooms make such integration a relatively easy task.

First, any good LMS allows for the integration of online library tutorials into courses. Such tutorials allow for students to complete library instruction at their own pace and can be easily customized for courses by requiring students to conduct library searches for specific assignments or projects. This both teaches critical skills and also incentivizes students to complete lessons that are immediately applicable to their courses. If extra motivation is still required, instructors can assign points to the tutorials and make them required parts of their courses.

Colleagues and I have done this in a pilot project within the entomology department at the University of Nebraska. The students were required to complete four online library modules: Getting Started with the Libraries, Creating Libraries Accounts, Conducting Research, and Avoiding Plagiarism. Each module included individual tutorials, with specific activities within the tutorials being related to their course, for a total of 15 tutorials. Completion of these modules was part of their overall course grade, and individual tutorials were required for completion of specific assignments, such as finding sources for their final research paper. During the entire course, the entomology librarian remained available to help students one-on-one and provide support when needed. The feedback from students has been highly positive, with many remarking that they wished they would have completed these tutorials earlier in their studies, and both the program director and entomology librarian were pleased with the improved ability of students to integrate the library's resources and services into their academic work. Consequently, the modules have been included in Insect Biology, a first-year undergraduate course, for Spring 2018, and additional modules are being planned for higher-level courses.

Second, a common feature of an LMS is the ability to add co-instructors or teaching assistants to an online course, so librarians themselves can integrated into courses. Librarians would welcome the opportunity to be made co-instructors of an online course. Making a librarian a co-instructor not only provides the benefit of an additional professional to help with instruction but also helps students view the librarian as an actual part of the course, not just an occasional visitor. This is critical if advanced information literacy skills, especially conducting research, are necessary for success in the course, as students are much more likely to seek out assistance from the librarian, leading to a much greater likelihood of success. Furthermore, this strengthens the relationship between instructor and librarian, which should lead to better instructional collaborations in the future. This should lead to better collaboration between the instructor and librarian to determine the extent to which the librarian would be involved in the course. For example, some instructors would be fully comfortable having librarians help develop and even teach instructional material, while others may prefer that the librarian develop and assess only library-related material. Either way, the fact that the librarian is now part of the course increases the likelihood that students make better use of library resources and services.

Finally, even if an instructor prefers to minimize the amount of coursework dedicated to library instruction, embedding library resources (e.g., the catalog, databases, librarian contact information) or linking to them is all it takes for students to recognize that the library is a valuable source of assistance in a course. Although this minimal approach reduces the chances that students will take full advantage of the resources and services offered through their institution's library, it still goes a long way to reducing the perception that the library is an optional part of an educational experience.

Four Copyright Questions to Ask before Posting Material in Your Online Classroom

Jillian R. Yarbrough and Robin E. Clark

YouTube videos, TED Talks, blogs, and journal articles. As faculty we have all these electronic resources and more available to us to share with our online students. But what copyright policies should we consider before we post an electronic resource to our LMS? This article offers a brief overview of the basics of copyright and how fair use is applied.

It is important to understand that, unlike a patent, a work is copyrighted as soon as it is created, provided the work is original and fixed in a tangible medium. There is no need to file any paperwork for copyright protection. By capturing your idea on a storyboard, in a paper, or with a video, you are protected by copyright. Why does this matter? Because it is important to understand that everything on the internet is copyrighted and owned by someone.

Now, as educators, we rely primarily on the doctrine of fair use to use copyrighted material in educational institutions for educational purposes, including in K–12 schools, colleges, and universities. Fair use is a statutory provision of the Copyright Act that makes the reasonable and limited use of copyrighted materials permissible without obtaining consent of the owner of the copyright. This means, in many cases, content that we find on the Internet can be used for instructional purposes if our use fits under the umbrella of fair use.

The Copyright Act gives four factors to consider when determining whether the use of a work will be considered fair use: (1) the purpose and character of the use, (2) the nature of the materials being used, (3) the amount and substantiality of the portion of the materials used in relation to the materials as a whole, and (4) the effect of the use on the value of the copyrighted materials. Unfortunately, there is no exact mathematical formula that we can use to determine whether our use of web-based materials will be fair under the Copyright Act. It is rather a matter of degree. Courts balance the number of "bad" factors against the number of "good" ones to determine whether the outcome is tipped toward the violation or nonviolation end of the spectrum. The best thing is to minimize the level of violation on each of the four factors.

To help you do so, we've crafted four questions to ask yourself before posting a resource in your online classroom.

1. **What is the purpose of the use?** It's important to consider whether the material will be used for commercial purposes or for nonprofit educational purposes. According to the U.S. Copyright Office (n.d.), courts examining the issue of fair use are more likely to find that nonprofit educational purposes fit the criteria of fair use than that commercial applications do. General guidelines permit an educator to make a copy of chapter from a book (other than a textbook), an article from a periodical, a short story, a short essay, a short poem, a chart, a graph, a diagram, a drawing, a cartoon, or a picture; with a notice of copyright affixed, the portion of the information can be shared with students. Educational publishers do not consider it fair use if the copying provides replacements or substitutes for the purchase of books, reprints, periodicals, tests, or other materials (Stim, 2019).
2. **Does your use of the materials transform or repurpose the materials for a new audience?** Generally, fair use can apply if the use is transformative. In other words, a work is transformed when the original material is modified by adding new expression, meaning, insights, or understandings. Pamela Samuelson (2009) has identified three categories that may be considered transformative under fair use: (1) transformative, creating new works that draw upon pre-existing work; (2) productive, using quotes or photographs or both for the purpose of writing a commentary; and (3) orthogonal, using copyright materials for a purpose different from the original one. Transformative use can include criticizing a quoted work, summarizing an idea in the original work to defend or rebut it, or creating a parody of the original work.
3. **How much of the materials are you using?** A third question concerns the amount of copyright material being used. To meet the

requirements of fair use, one should use the least amount of the material necessary to meet the educational need. The less material used, the more likely that the copying will be recognized as fair use. While in the past, many believed they would be protected under fair use if they were using fewer than 250 words or less than 10 percent of the work, there is no set number or percentage that guarantees fair use under all circumstances (DeVries, 2015). Certainly, the amount of material used matters, but the exact portion of the work also matters. For example, was the portion used the most significant or memorable part of the material? If the answer is yes, it may no longer be considered fair use. In other words, the amount used is measured not only quantitatively but also qualitatively. For example, a short clip from a movie is usually acceptable but possibly not acceptable if the segment encompasses the most extraordinary or creative elements of the film (Temple University, 2018).

4. **Will your use of the material cause a loss of money to the owner?** The fourth factor is whether your use deprives the copyright owner of income or undermines a new or potential market for the copyrighted work. Depriving a copyright owner of income will likely not be considered fair use. This is true even if you are not competing directly with the original work. For example, if an instructor copies parts of a textbook and sells the excerpts within a course packet so students no longer need to purchase the original text, this would result in loss of money for the owner and would not be considered fair use.

Ultimately, whether a work is considered fair use is determined solely by our courts. This means that even if educators do their best to reduce the amount of copyright infringement, the originators of materials may still raise concerns. But by being mindful of what courts look for to determine copyright infringement, educators can reduce their exposure while providing students with the benefit of the wealth of resources available on the Internet.

References

DeVries, H. (2015, July 22). What is fair when it comes to fair use? *Forbes*. https://www.forbes.com/sites/henrydevries/2015/07/22/what-is-fair-when-it-comes-to-fair-use/#311cc92b5134

Samuelson, P. (2009). Unbundling fair uses. *Fordham Law Review, 77*(5), 2537–2621. https://ir.lawnet.fordham.edu/flr/vol77/iss5/16

Stim, R. (2019). Educational uses of non-coursepack material. https://fairuse.stanford.edu/overview/academic-and-educational-permissions/non-coursepack

Temple University. (2018, August 13). Copyright for educators: A guide to the law and fair use. https://guides.temple.edu/c.php?g=348649&p=2351948

U.S. Copyright Office. (n.d.). More information on fair use. https://www.copyright.gov/fair-use/more-info.html

An Engagement Epidemic: Designing an Immersive, Media-Rich Course

Eric Yager and Tammy Garren

Long before the written word, humans relied on stories to entertain, instruct, and preserve cultural traditions. Storytelling is a fundamental way that humans communicate, and yet it is often left out of the college classroom. Rather than telling students stories about *how* something works or *why* it matters, too often faculty simply present them with PowerPoints that list *what* facts they need to remember and *when* that should occur.

In our online virology course, we combined storytelling with a simulation to encourage our students to construct knowledge and solve a real-world problem. Students played the part of apprentice virologists charged with solving a viral outbreak across campus by identifying the virus and the appropriate treatment and prevention. Our hope (and we're happy to say it worked) was to see the students think and communicate like virologists, weave discrete facts together to synthesize concepts, and collaborate in teams to address both the scientific and the societal fallout of disease.

We start the simulation with the following story:

> In a lab on the campus of a pharmacy school in upstate New York, a research assistant (who will remain unnamed) orders a shipment of specimens to be delivered to campus. As is the case with many young, ambitious researchers, this one is overworked and lacking sleep. While unpacking the specimens, the researcher discovers he's received unlabeled specimens resembling but not identical to those ordered. The researcher fumbles and the glass vials shatter, spilling the contents across the benchtop. Maintenance is called, the spill is isolated, and the researcher is evaluated by local doctors. In a statement to the press, the College reassures the public that "appropriate measures were taken

immediately to clean up the spill" and that "the researcher is expected to return to campus after a short recovery at home."

However, by the time this announcement is made dozens of people have come in direct contact with the spill. Without knowing much about the specimen or how infectious it is, no one knows how far or how fast illness will spread, how to prevent further spread, or how to treat those who have already come in contact. It's the job of students in BIO240 to gather clues, evaluate evidence, and work as a team to solve the outbreak.

Our outbreak story is broken into 13 short videos, each structured as newsroom updates from a fictitious local news station. Each newscast is coupled with on-the-scene footage and interviews with key players in the outbreak including concerned students, an infectious disease doctor, a recovering patient, and a local politician. These videos were designed to be filled with enough drama to keep the students engaged and sufficient realism to provide relevant connections to course material. The story of the outbreak will remain the same in future iterations of the course, though with a different virus each semester. Because we anticipated the need to change the mystery virus every year, videos were built to be open to interpretation. For instance, the patient interview included more information and symptoms than needed to pinpoint the virus (much like a typical patient encounter). This reinforced a skill our students will need in their professional careers.

How the course was designed

Building the course took three phases. In the first phase, we chose a virus, aligned our objectives, evaluated the content material and technological tools we would use, storyboarded the videos, and developed the course structure. We structured each week in the semester identically. Students were broken up into teams. Each team chose a name and members assigned themselves "superpowers" based on talents they thought may help in solving the outbreak—from the serious (being detail-oriented in deciphering clues) to the humorous (self-identifying as a genuine "patient zero" in infection outbreaks in their dorm!). Students were asked to complete a series of tasks: watch the viral outbreak video, watch the mini-lectures, read in the textbook and answer mastery quiz questions, participate in a discussion board, and complete group tasks.

In the second phase, we built the course and created the multimedia. Group tasks were selected based on objectives, time, and skills required. For each weekly module, groups were asked to complete tasks that allowed for creativity and critical thinking. Tasks included case studies, informative tables, patient information pamphlets, and illustrations. The summer before the course was available for enrollment, we filmed each week's episode. We recruited family, friends, and colleagues (who graciously worked for free) to serve as actors in our fictitious outbreak. We used technology and software owned by the college or donated by others (cameras; tripods; a green-screen room at a local middle school; Adobe Premiere, Photoshop, and After Effects; Camtasia; and Audacity). Content mini-lectures were also filmed over the summer using Panopto, video recording software integrated into our Blackboard LMS.

We researched and wrote discussion questions meant to challenge students' understanding of the science behind viruses by bringing in societal concerns. For instance, during the influenza module, students were asked to defend their stance on whether the devastation of the 1918 influenza pandemic was due to (1) the unique biology of the virus or (2) the historical context of World War I. Finally, clues to the identity of the virus were created in Adobe Photoshop and appeared as puzzle piece image files, which the students downloaded and assembled in Word as they earned them. These clues were built into our LMS using adaptive release (groups received clues upon receiving a grade of at least 85 percent on their weekly group work). The course culminated with students demonstrating their ability to communicate and apply knowledge as a virologist would by submitting a final report to the NDCA (our fictitious version of the Centers for Disease Control and Prevention) in which they identified the mystery virus, provided a treatment and prevention plan, and identified the information that led them to their recommendations.

In the third and final phase, we advertised and quality-checked the course. Two versions of posters were created and hung around campus with a QR code that brought students to a trailer for the course. The posters were effective: the course reached capacity within the first five minutes of course enrollment. On the back end, we clicked through the course and made sure students wouldn't encounter any issues on their quest to solve the outbreak.

Part 2 Redesigning a Course

Easy Steps to Revitalize Courses

Maryellen Weimer

It's the beginning of another academic year, and that means lots and lots of last-minute course preparation. Perhaps it's not the best time to propose course redesign projects, but how many course assignments, problem sets, exam formats, or paper topics haven't been changed for some time? The last time the syllabus was significantly revised was . . . when, exactly?

Faculty workloads are unquestionably heavy. But in a blog post several years ago, I proposed that busyness should not be a perennial excuse for avoiding course redesign projects, because there are ways to make those projects manageable. Here are some ideas:

- Take on one redesign project in one course per semester. Start with a list of everything within that course (or several courses, if you're feeling ambitious) that needs some updating or a new look. That's your master plan. Start with whatever is most motivating at the moment.
- Take any redesign project (a syllabus refresh with a more positive tone and different format, for example) and break the task into pieces—doable chunks that can be accomplished in modest time windows.
- Use what's redesigned for one course in other courses. If it's a new approach to quizzing, see whether it or some iteration of it works in a second course.
- Don't just focus on changing parts of the course that aren't working well. Look at what's working well and consider ways of doing that more in the course.
- Don't quest for "perfect" designs for exams, group projects, rubrics, online discussions, or any other aspects of instruction; they don't exist. The goal is to create learning experiences that promote content acquisition and skill development for the majority of students.

- Engage students in the process. Talk about what's being redesigned. Solicit their input and their feedback. Most will be impressed that they've been asked and happy to help.
- Doing some course redesign is better than doing none. There's always more that probably should be done, yes, but credit is deserved for what's being accomplished.
- For needed motivation, recognize that working on redesign projects—whether a new assignment or a different activity format—is an energizing process. It can add life to a course that may have become all too familiar.

Refresh Your Course: Step by Step

Rebecca Brent

You've decided you need to update, redesign, or refresh your course. Maybe you're doing so because of poor student performance. Perhaps you want to try a new technique or a tool. Or maybe your reasons are external, such as a change in the curriculum, new material, or a new text.

Most instructors simply don't have enough time to do everything we'd like to do in our teaching, including redesigning our courses. I'd like to share my process, which will allow you to be systematic about how you go about changing your course, keeping it fresh for you and for your students—and letting learning happen the way you intend it to.

STEP 1: Identify your reason(s) for changing the course

What is it that makes you think you need to do something to the class? The more clearly you focus on the reason for the change, the easier it is to figure out what direction you want to go.

There are many possibilities. Here are some common ones:

- *Student performance is not where you want it to be.* Maybe students are weak in a particular topic or skill, or their performance throughout the course is failing to meet your expectations.
- *Some course content is obsolete.* Curriculum revisions or other program changes may have changed the course objectives, or you may realize that the content is simply outdated.
- *A new text has been chosen.* New texts often require changing the order in which course content is presented and possibly the content itself.
- *You have learned about new teaching techniques or tools.* Powerful instructional technology tools, for example, appear with increasing frequency.

- *You or the students (or both) are bored, and you want to liven up the course.* It's easy to get burned out on a course after teaching it a number of times. Changing the course can increase your motivation and energy, and your renewed energy can help energize the students.

Spend some time with step one, because that will target your action. Sometimes people jump too quickly to simply find new resources. And they haven't really thought about what the issue is that they're trying to address.

STEP 2: Gather ideas and resources

Once you have determined your motivation to change, consider which features of the course you want to change and how changing them will address the problem(s) you've identified. Then use some of the following strategies to begin putting a plan together:

- *Reflect on student feedback.* Look at student comments from the last times you taught the course to get ideas about how to make the course better.
- *Discuss your course concerns with others and collect and evaluate ideas.* Experienced colleagues and teaching center staff members are good sources. By the end of this step, you should begin to identify teaching resources that might be useful in your revision.
- *Evaluate teaching resources.* The internet is a treasure trove of resources, many of which you can download and use at no cost. Online material such as class session plans, handouts, photos, videos, screencasts, simulations, case studies, and interactive tutorials can be found using general digital resource libraries (e.g., MERLOT, Wikimedia Commons, Google Images, the National Science Digital Library) or enter "[type of resource][topic]" into a search engine to find subject-specific resources.

STEP 3: Plan the changes

This is the fun part! Step three involves actually deciding on ideas. What are you going to do? Think about deciding on a change and then making a schedule for that.

It could be short and sweet—something simple like adding new readings. Or it could be big, like flipping your class. It is easy to get overwhelmed. It is a huge job to completely flip your class. Most people find that they can manage it much better if they take an incremental approach. The idea is to make those major changes gradually.

Once you decide on the specific changes you want to make, lay out a schedule for making them. There are a number of things you might do, depending on the kind of changes you're considering. Here are just a few of them:

- *Add connections between course content and students' interests and prior knowledge.* (This suggestion is discussed in detail later.)
- *Begin or increase instruction in metacognition, critical thinking, or creative thinking.* An example of the gradual incorporation of self-regulated learning strategies, metacognition, and critical thinking in a sociology course is given in Pelton, J. A. (2014). How our majors believe they learn: Student learning strategies in an undergraduate theory course. *Teaching Sociology, 42*(4), 277–286.
- *Update an assignment.* An excellent description of a change from journaling assignments to blogging in a marketing class is Muncy, J. A. (2014). Blogging for reflection: The use of online journals to engage students in reflective learning. *Marketing Education Review, 24*(2), 101–113.
- *Incorporate technology into course instruction.* Resources and where to find them are listed in step 2.
- *Use pre-class quizzes to encourage students to read material and to give them retrieval practice on key information and concepts.*
- *If your course involves selecting materials as bases for instruction and discussion (e.g., readings in a language or literature course), introduce new selections.*
- *Use active learning* to enhance students' knowledge acquisition and skill development—including critical and creative thinking skills—and to reduce their boredom and yours. (This point is also discussed later.)
- *Use case studies* to make course material more relevant to important social issues and students' interests. An excellent listing of resources on case study teaching is available here: https://sciencecases.lib.buffalo.edu/collection.
- *Develop group assignments* using structured cooperative learning to promote skill development—including critical and creative thinking, communication, and teamwork skills—and reduce grading loads in large classes. A chapter on the basics of working with groups can be found here: https://www.engr.ncsu.edu/wp-content/uploads/drive/1PLmbl9qPHpwYV7GFqUgWTHm5YNDzHV8V/2007-CL-Chapter.pdf.
- *Flip your classroom.* Use online assignments to give students their first exposure to course content, and then in class actively engage them in

applying the content to solve problems, analyze readings and cases, discuss important points, and so on.

What follows are tips for increasing the effectiveness of course modifications.

Use learning objectives to guide your changes

Learning objectives are statements of actions students may take to demonstrate whether and how well they have learned what you have attempted to teach. Objectives begin with a concrete, observable action verb, such as *list, explain, calculate, construct, deconstruct, derive, prove, critique, formulate*, and *design*. (Avoid words like *know, learn, understand*, and *appreciate*—such actions are not directly observable.) Think of objectives as anything you might ask students to do on an assignment or test.

Try to formulate a fairly complete set of learning objectives for the course you are redesigning, and once you have them, use them to guide all of the changes you make—adding, modifying, and deleting content; designing assignments, projects, and tests; and changing teaching methods and tools. When examining content, distinguish between "need to know" material (which directly addresses your objectives) and "nice to know" material (which doesn't), and focus on the former. An introduction to objectives is given here (https://www.engr.ncsu.edu/stem-resources/legacy-site/education-related-papers/learning-objectives-intro), and additional resources can be found on the CTL sites at Iowa State (http://www.celt.iastate.edu/teaching/preparing-to-teach/tips-on-writing-course-goalslearning-outcomes-and-measureable-learning-objectives) and Carnegie Mellon (http://www.celt.iastate.edu/teaching/preparing-to-teach/tips-on-writing-course-goalslearning-outcomes-and-measureable-learning-objectives).

Connect content to students' interests and prior knowledge

Cognitive science has shown that students don't learn by receiving brand new information and inserting it directly into their long-term memories. Instead, they learn by integrating new information with related material in their long-term memories. The more we activate their prior knowledge (i.e., help them remember related information) and give them chances to make sense of the new material themselves, the more likely they will be to learn it. Here are several ways to do it:

- Ask students on day 1 to list questions they have about course topics and things they'd like to learn.
- Challenge students to find real-world applications of course topics to

current issues and their personal interests.
- Use graphic organizers to help students integrate what they know with what they are learning and to organize the combined material in a way that makes sense.
- Give students choice in course readings, project topics, and other aspects of the course.

Use active learning

> Learning is not a spectator sport. Students do not learn much just by sitting in class listening to teachers, memorizing prepackaged assignments, and spitting out answers. They must talk about what they are learning, write about it, relate it to past experiences, apply it to their daily lives. They must make what they learn part of themselves.
> —Arthur W. Chickering and Zelda F. Gamson, "Seven Principles for Good Practice in Undergraduate Education," *AAHE Bulletin*, March 1987

Active learning is anything course-related students do in class other than watch the teacher and take notes. An activity can be done by individuals, groups of two to four students, or students who first work alone then pair up to synthesize their ideas' with others (*think-pair-share*). The instructor asks a question or poses a problem and gives individual students or student teams from as little as 10 seconds to as much as three minutes (rarely longer) to do something. The activity might be to

- recall prior material;
- answer or generate a question;
- explain a concept in their own words;
- translate or interpret a passage of prose or poetry;
- start or work out the next step in a problem solution, derivation, or case study analysis;
- think of an example or application of a method taught in class;
- figure out why a predicted outcome turned out to be wrong;
- brainstorm a list (the goal is quantity, not quality); or
- summarize a lecture.

The instructor stops the activity after the allotted time and randomly calls on one or more students for their responses, or sometimes calls for volunteers. *This activity works for all class levels and sizes.*

Active learning is a great strategy for getting students to engage with challenging material and practice skills. If you're concerned about weak student performance, consider using active learning.

The following references provide more information about active learning:

- Felder, M., & Brent, R. (2009, August). Active learning: An introduction. *ASQ Higher Education Brief, 2*(4). http://asq.org/edu/2009/08/best-practices/active-learning-an-introduction.%20felder.pdf
  - A short paper that defines active learning, gives examples of activities and formats, and answers frequently asked questions about the method.
- Prather, E., Rudolph, A., & Brissenden, G. (2011, Summer). Using research to bring interactive learning strategies into general education mega-courses. *Peer Review, 13*(3). https://www.aacu.org/publications-research/periodicals/using-research-bring-interactive-learning-strategies-general
  - Classes that spent 25 percent of their class time or more using active strategies averaged more than double the normalized gains of classes that spent 25 percent or less, independent of class size (which was as large as 800 students).
- Richard Felder. (2015, June 29). *Creating partnerships: Active learning in an engineering class* [Video]. YouTube. https://www.youtube.com/watch?v=0p7gNXGvcww
  - A 32-minute video on YouTube containing clips of Dr. Richard Felder using active learning in a large class, with narration by Dr. Felder and Dr. Rebecca Brent and post-course comments from several of the students about the impact of the teaching method on their learning.
- The University of Pittsburgh's Center for Teaching and Learning. (n.d.). Designing in-class activities: Examples of active learning activities. https://teaching.pitt.edu/wp-content/uploads/2018/12/GSTI-Designing_In-Class_Activities-Handout-Examples_Of_Active_Learning_Activities.pdf

Make major changes gradually

The greater the change you propose to make, the more likely you are to be uncomfortable, make mistakes, and encounter student pushback. Remember that whatever changes you make don't have to be completed in one term. If you'd like to make a big change (like flipping your classroom), consider making it gradually over several terms so you never venture far outside your comfort zone. As your confidence builds, you can apply the changes to more and more of the course.

The following plan for flipping a classroom can be adapted to any major course change you might want to make.

Illustrative plan for flipping a class

SUMMER	• Identify one or two topics for flipping. • Collect or develop short video clips and screencasts (about 6 minutes in length and no more than 10 minutes) and other online resources. • Develop a strategy for getting students to do the online assignments and plans for what you and the students will do in class (e.g., active learning exercises, computer assignments)
FALL	• Try the course with the flipped topics and take notes on what works and what doesn't. • Ask for student feedback on the flipped topics.
WINTER BREAK	• Adjust the topics to address problems and suggestions from students.
SPRING	• Teach the modified course.
SUMMER	• Identify two additional topics for flipping and repeat the sequence.

STEP 4: Plan the evaluation

When you change a course, the one thing you can be sure of is that you won't get it right the first time. Before you implement the changes, it's important to have an evaluation plan in place that you will use to determine the effects of the changes. Use the plan to help you determine which changes to keep, which ones to modify, and which ones to drop next time you teach the course. Here is how you might formulate your plan.

- *Decide whether you want to carry out a formal or informal evaluation.* If you are making significant and costly changes, are making small changes that you might scale up if the results are promising, or plan to publish conclusions about the effect of specific changes on students' performance or retention, you should conduct a formal evaluation that rigorously determines the effects of the changes. In cases in which none of those conditions apply, an informal evaluation based on students' survey responses and your impressions about changes in their performance should be adequate.
- *Informal evaluation.* Collect midterm evaluations that specifically ask students whether they believe the new or modified features of the course helped their learning, hindered their learning, or did neither. If you can include similar questions on the end-of-course

evaluations, do so. While the course is in progress, note any improvements (or lack thereof) you see in students' performance and attitudes in areas targeted by the changes.

- *Formal evaluation.* Decide on the measures you will assess to evaluate the effects of your changes, such as grades on assignments, project reports, tests or test items, surveys, and observations. Either carry out a study in which the assessment results for students in the modified course are compared with the results for a matched group of students taking the original course, or teach the course once before making the changes and again with the changes and compare the assessment results for students in both course offerings. (For more details on carrying out such action research studies, see here: http://celt.ust.hk/teaching-resources/action-research.)

STEP 5: Implement the changes and evaluate the outcomes

Carry out the plans formulated in steps 3 and 4. Examine the results, and use them to plan what, if anything, you will change the next time you teach the course.

STEP 6: Regularly reflect on the course and how you are teaching it

All teachers should have a goal of continuing to grow and improve their teaching. Here are ways to do it in the course we have been discussing, assuming that nothing dramatic has happened to make major changes necessary. (In such cases, go back to Step 1.)

After each class session: In your office immediately after a session, spend a few minutes going through the session plan and reflecting on which lecture segments, questions, and activities went the way you had in mind; which didn't; and what changes you will make next time you teach the course. Jot the changes down on the session plan, and prepare revised plans for all sessions before you teach the course again. After you've taught the course two or three times following this procedure, the session plans should be close to where you would like them to be.

At the end of the term: After the course is over; assignments, projects, exams have been given and graded; and evaluations have been collected from students and faculty colleagues, spend an hour or so going over all of it and reflecting on how you think things went. Then make notes on your syllabus and other course materials about what you want to do differently next time, and carry out those changes when the time comes.

Adapted from the Magna Online Seminar presentation *Refresh Your Course with Straightforward Design Changes*, 2015.

Keep Calm and Redesign with Perspective

Bridget Arend

Sometimes we are asked to step during an emergency situation when a colleague cannot finish teaching a course. Sometimes enrollment or structural changes mean we are unexpectedly assigned to take on a new course just days before the semester starts. And sometimes, beyond our wildest imaginations, a pandemic causes us to reformat our on-campus courses for online delivery overnight.

All these options are far from ideal. As someone who regularly helps faculty thoughtfully redesign their courses, I know that quality course design takes time. Ideally, we want any redesign process to involve rethinking assumptions; developing a clear sense of overall goals; considering internal and external expectations; and tinkering (sometimes excessively) with content, resources, assignments, and instructional activities. A thorough course redesign is best completed when you have carved out some time and space for fresh thinking. But what do we do without the luxury of time?

If you're currently teaching a course that needs to be retooled, restructured, or redesigned midstream, here are a few things to keep your expectations realistic and your sanity intact.

Focus on long-term goals

In an unexpected course redesign situation, many questions are going to emerge before you have the time to think them through. Can students complete alternative assignments? What if a student misses an essential component of the course? What if your final exam or class presentations need to occur online? At this point we can borrow some lessons from the established course design models, such as integrated course design (Fink, 2013) and backward design processes (Wiggins & McTighe, 2011). It is immensely valuable to have a clear mental picture of our end goal.

While we may be tempted to start planning what needs to happen tomorrow, taking even just 20 minutes to breathe, step back, and write out the long-term goals for student learning can help us make the right decisions in the short term. What do you hope that students will carry with them long after completing this course? What impact do you want this course—or the current situation—to have on their lives? These are not small questions, but the clearer our intentions and purposes are from the outset, the easier it will be to make those "in the moment" decisions.

Remember that less is more

The benefits of "depth over breadth" approaches to teaching provide value for any course but are especially important when the time frame changes. We may have to face the reality that we simply cannot do everything we want to do in the course and that trying to "get it all in" may actually do more harm than good. Instead, take solace in the value of going deeper in learning—perhaps less reading, less content, and more focus on connections, reflection, and application. Carefully consider what is essential to accomplishing those long-term goals, what could be left out, and ultimately where you want your students to focus their limited time and energy.

Involve the students

Students can be incredibly supportive and understanding when given the chance. If they know you are doing your best and have their long-term interests at heart, they are often very willing to work with you. Share your long-term goals with them and discuss your planned changes. What if they tried to write the course learning outcomes, in their own words and in ways that make sense given their situations, or even create their own learning plans? Discuss why what they learn in this class matters—or better yet, ask them to make this connection themselves. Why not ask for their suggestions at how best to achieve the learning goals? They may uncover some creative options or find their own technology solutions. You don't have to adopt every idea, but they may come up with some great options, and you'll gain valuable student buy-in through the process.

Give yourself a break

These are far from ideal situations, and no one can expect perfection. We may even make mistakes—add in too many activities, focus on the wrong resources, or set up a new project that fails. These are mistakes to learn from! Yes, if we had more time, we could do some truly wonderful things. But we can also appreciate the small steps we've taken to support meaningful learning. Be patient, and be kind and gracious to yourself and your students. Keep your eyes on those long-term goals, and celebrate small achievements along the way!

References

Fink, L. D. (2013). *Creating significant learning experiences: An integrated approach to designing college courses* (2nd ed.). John Wiley & Sons.

Wiggins, G. P., & McTighe, J. (2011). *The understanding by design guide to creating high-quality units.* ASCD.

Refresh Your Course with Open Educational Resources

Olena Zhadko and Susan Ko

Many faculty and institutions are turning to open educational resources (OER) to lower costs to students and improve instruction. While much has been written about the search, evaluation, and selection process for OER, the need to produce a coherent and engaging design for OER delivery often goes unmentioned. Redesigning a course with OER requires time, planning, and expertise in course design.

This process is best guided with a plan for evaluating the current course and incorporating OER into the design.

First, find out whether support is offered on your campus. Libraries, centers for teaching and learning, and offices of online education would be the places to consult with. This is important because in addition to pure OER (both those licensed as such and works in the public domain), there are free materials available to students through institutions (for example, library subscriptions) and other agencies.

Many online educators mix and match OER and other free materials because sometimes it is simply not possible to use OER alone. You may then deploy your own lecture materials and commentaries to illuminate, enhance, and fill in any gaps in the coverage of topics.

Second, learn whether colleagues at your institution are adopting or creating OER and inquire about their work. These colleagues can provide ideas about how different resources integrate into the institution's learning management system, students' perceptions of the resources, and how to make the most of existing resources and available services to redesign your course with OER.

Third, conduct an inventory of existing learning materials. List all materials required for each week of the course, noting those you are potentially targeting for replacement by OER. Use our OER Course Planning Document (http://celt.ust.hk/teaching-resources/action-research) to guide this process. As you work with this document, make sure you select just one course to start with—ideally, one that already utilizes free materials. You even can try using the name of the course in your search for OER.

During the initial search you may want to look for an open textbook. Review the list of criteria in the OER Course Planning Document for the essential elements to guide you. Additionally, you might use a rubric to evaluate any open textbooks you do find. For example, Affordable Learning Georgia offers an easy-to-use rubric with guiding questions (https://www.affordablelearninggeorgia.org/find_textbooks/selecting_textbooks).

Compare a few textbooks. Note that you can mix and match chapters, sections, and additional resources from several sources, which will require additional work on your part. Of course, if you are able to find one open textbook that meets your needs, you can consider yourself lucky!

If you cannot find an open textbook, search for curated material for your subject. Remember to go beyond Google and make full use of OER repositories. For example, SUNY Geneseo's OASIS (https://oasis.geneseo.edu/index.php) and OER Commons (https://www.oercommons.org/oer) provide rich repositories. As you make your initial search, take notes on your findings.

After the initial search, start working on the week-by-week OER Course Planning Document. Take an inventory of your course, and note the areas that will need attention, changes, or revisions. Following the path outlined in the document, identify your learning units, weeks, and modules. Whether it's an accelerated six-week course or a regular 15-week course, it is important to fill this out diligently and pay close attention to the licensing conditions of the new learning materials you will adopt. While completing this exercise, you may discover that some of the content you use in your course does not relate to your unit's learning outcomes. You can then either discard it or revise learning outcomes to ensure that they reflect the intended learning for the course.

If you are unable to find OER learning materials, you may need to create your own. As you do, consider making them OER and assigning appropriate licenses as well as contributing them to an OER repository such as MERLOT (https://www.merlot.org/merlot/index.htm).

Once you have completed the week-by-week planning document, go back to the beginning and note the rationale for selecting your OER. Then use this completed planning document to revise your course. You will want to create a comprehensive project plan, adding a column for due dates and perhaps another for checking off each section as it is built out on your chosen platform.

If you would like additional guidance about search, evaluation, and planning or happen to lead OER faculty development at your institution, explore this website (https://oerworkshop.commons.gc.cuny.edu), which provides information about and the content for a two-week faculty workshop. This workshop is itself an OER, offering a deep dive into OER and showing faculty how to find, evaluate, and integrate OER into their courses with intentional course design.

Course Redesign: A Compelling Example

Maryellen Weimer

Many of our course revisions happen without much planning. A new idea comes down the pike, an interesting technology option becomes available, a colleague shares a strategy that effectively deals with an issue, and we just use it! So the course evolves and changes but not all that systematically. As a result, most of the change happens at the margins. That's not bad, but it does not result in transformational change. It's not change that steers the course in a whole new direction. That much change makes most faculty nervous. It requires considerable work and often entails using teaching practices outside their current comfort zone.

What we need are good examples of how big changes can be implemented incrementally and iteratively. And the article highlighted here contains such an example.

An upper-division neurophysiology course, enrolling between 80 and 110 students, was redesigned over four years (with fine-tuning still going on). It started out as a traditional lecture course with familiar problems. The instructor wanted students to apply course concepts in new situations and to develop thinking that was more expert-like, but the students were into memorizing: "In many cases, students could only reproduce information from lecture" (Casagrand & Semsar, 2017, p. 195). To try to improve students' ability to apply the content, the instructor decided to implement some evidence-based active learning approaches. The course's content was not changed. The instructor started out by creating homework assignments that gave students practice working with concepts they struggled with on the exams. The assignments started out short and involved lower-order cognitive skills, such as the vocabulary students needed to answer higher-order questions. Students responded positively, and three years later the number and level of questions had increased; the homework was due weekly and counted for 15 percent of students' grades.

After the addition of the homework assignments, the instructor started using clicker questions once, sometimes twice, per class session. On the basis of more favorable student response, the instructor increased the number so that they were now used between two and six times per class session and involved mostly higher-order questions.

Perhaps most interesting: to encourage students to work together on homework assignments, the instructor created an informal, optional homework help room that was available for several hours the day before the homework was due. Students could help each other; a TA was available, and sometimes the teacher was.

As the revision proceeded, the instructor introduced learning goals that made explicit what students were expected to know and to be able to do. As a result of this set of changes, the course exams gradually changed so that by the end of the four-year revision period, only 14 percent of the exam questions remained the same. The content hadn't changed, but the questions now asked students to demonstrate a conceptual understanding of the material. The questions also more closely aligned with the homework, clicker questions, and course learning goals. She also worked to maintain exam averages, thereby certifying the rigor of the course content.

Another factor makes this course revision a great example. When the instructor started making these changes, she, like most teachers, wasn't thinking about how she was going to assess them. She gathered no baseline data. But with this many revisions involving this much work, she really needed to know whether the reform was worth the effort. She did have class responses to 12 test questions used before and after the course redesign. She then developed a unique way to use Bloom's taxonomy to assess changes in the cognitive levels of the exams. The results of this analysis confirmed that these course revisions were well worth the effort. On the exam questions used before and after the revisions, student performance was significantly higher in the post-reform semester, rising from 59 percent to 76 percent. Students answered more of the lower- and higher-order questions correctly. The revised course exams had double the number of higher-order questions. There was also improvement for both higher- and lower-performing students.

Student responses to the reforms were positive: "Although students may not be best at recognizing what helps them learn or in assessing their true level of understanding, student attitudes are an indicator of student buy-in to teaching strategies" (p. 200). The most compelling example was student use of the optional help room. Seventy percent reported using it, and of those who used it, 93 percent said they worked with peers while there.

Before the revisions, an estimated 10–20 percent of the students came to instructor and TA office hours.

Finally, there's a thoughtful analysis of what made this revision a success. First, the authors point to the inclusion of multiple active learning strategies and the fact they were implemented incrementally, which allowed them to be improved as the revisions moved forward. Second, the course's goals and formative and summative assessments were tightly aligned. Students knew what they needed to know and be able to do, and they had the opportunity to practice and receive feedback before the exam. Third, students were on board. They recognized that what they were experiencing in class was improving their learning and their performance. Lastly, the instructor lacked departmental support in the beginning, but as the project moved forward, the department formed an association with a science education initiative project that provided various kinds of support.

It was a best-case scenario with a variety of factors aligning for the success. Unfortunately, for many faculty barriers to implementing these kinds of substantive changes are present. Nonetheless, there is still much to be learned from this example of course redesign.

Reference

Casagrand, J., & Semsar, K. (2017). Redesigning a course to help students achieve higher-order cognitive thinking skills: From goals and mechanics to student outcomes. *Advances in Physiology Education, 41*(2), 194–202. https://doi.org/10.1152/advan.00102.2016

A Checklist for Moving Your Course Online

Angela Heath

A checklist is absolutely essential to moving a face-to-face course online. It not only enables the instructor conceptualize their course in an online environment but also helps the instructional designer see what needs to be done. Here is a simple guide to preparing to move your courses online.

Topics to consider

Course length and time frame

Most courses run the length of a semester, but this does not always translate directly to an online format. For instance, you may have 30 minutes of instruction in a course session followed by class activity and homework. Students are then given activities and readings to do outside of class that support the lecture. By contrast, in an online course, the "lecture" need not be the center of instruction, but more of a means to guide students to the concepts they will learn through other material. In my online business courses, I like to first provide students with relevant practical materials so they can dive in and see the concepts in action. I then use my lecture as a way to wrap up and highlight what was learned in the module.

Course objectives

In many cases, there are fewer course objectives for online courses in that material is chunked to keep students from becoming overwhelmed. Review current course objectives and make a note of which topics contain the most and the least number of objectives. Also, make a note of which topics, modules, and sessions contain objectives that are often difficult for your students.

Learning activities

Some of the biggest misconceptions are made when considering learning activities. For instance, many faculty believe that the online course equivalent involves simply uploading PowerPoint slides to substitute for in-class lectures. In face-to-face classes, learning activities often consist of lecture, discussions, practice problems, discussion, group work, and so on. Of course, this can greatly depend on the subject being taught, the size of the class, the comfort level of the teacher, the available technology in the room, and many other things.

Assessments

Does your course have a midterm and a final? How about weekly quizzes, homework, lab assignments, and practice problem sets? How do these translate into an online environment? There are many ways to handle assessments, but you need to be clear on whether the assessment is a formative or summative one. A formative assessment gauges how students are doing along the way. The purpose of a formative assessment is to provide feedback and inform students of their progress and what they need to improve upon. By contrast, summative assessments are more final and should be used to evaluate students on their level of learning, skills development, and overall achievement in the course. The type of assessment will help you determine the appropriate online strategy to access your students.

Course development checklist for faculty

Now that you've thought about your course in both formats—face-to-face and the new online format—you will need to succinctly summarize this for your instructional designer. It is helpful to have a checklist that summarizes the major aspects of your face-to-face course before you sit down with your instructional designer. This ensures that you both are on the same page about the course structure, learning activities, assessments, and so on.

Below are the questions to answer when filling out your checklist.

Overall course features

- What are the top three features that you MOST like about your course? In other words, which course features (lectures, exams, assignments, etc.) do you feel work, and would you keep these the same?
- What are the top three features that you LEAST like about your course? In other words, which features (lectures, exams, assignments, etc.) would you change if you could?
- Which two course features (lectures, exams, assignments, etc.) do you feel work, and would you keep these the same?

Learning activities

- What are the three MOST popular learning activities in your course (e.g., the wiki on green computing)?
- What are two challenges or struggles have you experienced in teaching this course? (Example: "Lecture two is dry, and students do not pick up the material well.")
- For students, what are the muddiest points per module or lecture in your course?
- What are three technology features that you would add to your course to enhance its learning activities?

Assessments

- Do you use any formative assessment tools, such as quizzes, homework, or practice sets? If yes, what are students required to do to successfully complete them?
- Do you have grading rubrics for your assessments?

Interactivity

- What are the three or four primary ways that students interact with you or with each other in your course?
- What are three or four interactions that you would like to see in an online course?
- The answers to these questions will guide your course development and will help your instructional designer translate your material to an online environment. Feel free to download a course development checklist here: https://bit.ly/2IeRn2K.
-

Successful online courses are carefully planned learning experiences with activities intended to encourage, engage, and empower students to learn independently. The main goal is to ensure that the intent, tone, and academic rigor of the course does not get lost in translation. Putting in a bit of legwork beforehand and thinking about the learning experience is crucial to ensuring a quality outcome.

Part 3 Constructing the Syllabus

Syllabi: Leveling the Playing Field

Jeanne M. Slattery

I'm a big fan of syllabi used well. On the crassest level—and it's important—syllabi are contracts between faculty and students, contracts that administration holds us to. When a student makes a complaint, administrators want to be able to pull out the course syllabus and use it to determine whether the faculty member has followed the rules as outlined in the syllabus (Slattery & Carlson, 2005).

The syllabus is my students' first impression of me, and it matters. Even half a minute of a video of a professor teaching predicts end-of-course student evaluations, even when that video is played without sound (Ambady & Rosenthal, 1993). That predictive power should not surprise us. By the time our students meet us, they've spent years with good teachers and bad and can quickly figure out which faculty and classes will best serve their needs.

Although syllabi identify necessary course rules and tasks, they also serve more altruistic and high-minded purposes. As I write a syllabus, I consider my course goals and how we as a class will go about meeting them (Slattery & Carlson, 2005). These goals provide the structure I need to organize the course, and they give my students something to strive for. I spend time thinking about how I can shape my syllabus to help students identify and use the strategies that make success in the course more likely. I strive to level the playing field for students who otherwise would be at a disadvantage (Collins, 1997). What makes sense to me may not make sense to students unless I communicate clearly and intentionally throughout the syllabus. I attend to tone and consider what I can do to engage my students in an effective partnership with me (Richmond et al., 2017). In sum, well-designed syllabi are opportunities to create engagement and success—for faculty, students, and the course.

What should we consider?

The nuts and bolts of syllabus design are discussed much more extensively elsewhere (see Gannon, 2019). At a minimum, effective syllabi include basic course information (e.g., name and prerequisites), required texts and readings, assignments, grades, and university policies. In this discussion, I want to focus on the motivational aspects of a syllabus: its tone, strategies for success, accessibility, and our students' meaning and purpose. These I see as the aspects of a syllabus that level the playing field and increase the likelihood that all students will succeed in the course.

Syllabus tone

Syllabus tone influences how our students perceive the course and us. Does your syllabus communicate low expectations and focus on punitive rules, or does it demonstrate that you expect success? Are students discussed as objects or partners? A positive syllabus tone removes barriers to learning and creates expectations that the course is a comfortable and safe place for learning.

My colleagues and I have been studying tone in learner-centered and teacher-centered syllabi for the past 10 years. Learner-centered syllabi build a sense of community, communicate a shared sense of power and control, and use student-centered strategies for evaluation. They are opposite in this focus to teacher-centered syllabi, which do not build community or share power or evaluation strategies (Cullen & Harris, 2009; Richmond et al., 2019). Interestingly, syllabus tone does not affect students' perceptions of a professor's knowledge, competence, or preparedness, but it does affect their attitudes toward the professor and course. Students reading more learner-centered syllabi perceive faculty as more flexible, open-minded, creative, and interesting. Faculty with learner-centered syllabi are seen by students as being caring, having positive attitudes, and being enthusiastic. Students rated a learner-centered syllabus much more positively than a teacher-centered syllabus and reported much higher levels of course engagement (Richmond et al., 2017).

Here's an example of a section from my online abnormal psychology syllabus that illustrates how I work to communicate the learner-centered notions of community and shared power identified by Cullen and Harris (2009). This respect for the unspoken experiences of others and the confidentiality of clients is particularly important in the online environment. Rather than being defensive in tone or setting up confrontations, my goal is to create a collaborative discussion. I have the same goals for my face-to-face courses, but the context does make a difference. I don't share my photo or schedule virtual office hours in those courses.

Let's Talk About Ethics . . .

Many of you plan on entering one of the helping professions (e.g., sociology/psychology, rehabilitative sciences, premed, nursing, education, special education). Given this—and our content—it is especially important for us to begin practicing ethical behavior. We should assume that someone "in the room" either deals with these issues personally or has someone close to them who does. Please ask questions to expand your understanding but recognize that course content may be personally sensitive for your classmates. Please use person-first language, protect people's privacy, talk about people in respectful manners, and listen to and respect other ideas. You don't need to agree with everyone else—you may often disagree—but you need to continue to find ways to respectfully and professionally disagree (e.g., using good listening skills, backing up your opinions with strong evidence).

For my part, I promise to listen carefully, encourage critical thinking about the topics we discuss, and work to build a safe, thoughtful, and respectful classroom. I will disguise the identity of the people in my cases and maintain their privacy, ask for my clients' consent before I talk about them with you, consider other explanations of symptoms, and stay current in my reading of the literature.

Strategies for success

I know what it takes to succeed in my courses, but many students may not. For years, I have included a list of strategies for performing well. More recently, I've also begun including what I call "pro tips" in my abnormal psychology syllabus. A bit more focused than my list of strategies for performing well, they are part of my goal to get students thinking and acting like the professionals they will soon be. Here are a couple of examples:

Pro Tip: You get the most out of assignments when you make them your own. What do you want to learn? Where do you need help?

Pro Tip: Getting to know and trust each other helps groups become more successful—and is especially important for online courses. Talk to each other regularly about class and "off-task" things too. Find methods that work for your group.

Inclusiveness

In several ways, syllabi can communicate that a class is relevant or irrelevant to students. Kuh (2009) found that students were more likely to perform at a high academic level when they perceived themselves to be members of a supportive learning community. Syllabi can include content that makes it clear that there's a place for everyone in the course. They do so through course goals and learning objectives, the course topics and readings included in the course, and statements that promote diversity. Students judged syllabi with diversity statements as creating a more favorable classroom climate; this was especially true when that statement appeared early in the syllabus (Stein, 2019). Here's how I try to make students feel welcome in my Abnormal Psychology syllabus. The text appears on my syllabus right below my contact information:

> **Welcome!** I'm glad you're here! I want this place to be a safe place for people of all ages, backgrounds, beliefs, ethnicities, genders, sexual identities, races, religions, and other visible and invisible differences. Together, we can create a respectful, welcoming, and inclusive place for all of us to work and learn in.

Accessibility

Faculty regularly accommodate students with disabilities. Many of these accommodations are services that we can offer *all* students to help them become more successful, regardless of whether they have given us a request from disability services. For example, my university's learning management system (D2L) has recently added docReader, which reads documents in D2L to students. docReader will obviously help students with learning disabilities and recent concussions, but other students may also find it helpful. I point out this feature and encourage all students to consider using it. Rather than tell only anxious students how to manage the course well, I tell *all* my students how to handle anxiety and the course effectively. I offer help proactively, not only when students request it. Requiring that students request services advantages those students who are more assertive or less anxious about revealing an invisible disability.

Of course, there are accommodations that I don't spontaneously offer to all students; I don't have time and energy to offer everyone testing in a quiet place, for example. When students ask, however, I consider strategies that meet their needs. I want the syllabus to clearly communicate my willingness to do what I can to help students have successful learning experiences in my courses.

Students' meaning and purpose

Our students have a long history of having their goals and sense of purpose ignored, so many see their assignments as busywork. We know better, but students may need some help in recognizing that assignments are purposefully designed and can be meaningful for them. I prompt students to find meaning and purpose in my assignments, as in this media analysis assignment in my forensic psychology course. I also use pro tips to get students thinking about how and why an assignment might be relevant to them.

> **Why this assignment?** The ability to think critically and question what you read and see is an important skill that will benefit you in many different parts of your life, not just your understanding of the court and prison systems. This assignment will help you build this important skill.

I also try to make assignments meaningful by identifying the relationships between learning goals and assignments in my syllabi. I try to be clear about the progression of assignments across the semester and identify how earlier assignments build success with later assignments. Some of these things are apparent in the syllabus.

Conclusion

Syllabi do not only meet contractual demands. They're an opportunity to help our students succeed in their courses and in life. Because I also see my syllabi as social justice tools, I continually consider how I can engage and motivate my students through them. I do this in the syllabus by working to communicate clearly that I'm committed to helping all students obtain the skills they need to succeed. I want them to recognize that I am their ally in and out of class.

References

Ambady, N., & Rosenthal, R. (1993). Half a minute: Predicting teacher evaluations from thin slices of nonverbal behavior and physical attractiveness. *Journal of Personality and Social Psychology, 64*(3), 431–441. https://doi.org/10.1037/0022-3514.64.3.431

Collins, T. (1997). For openers . . . An inclusive syllabus. In W. E. Campbell and K. A. Smith (Eds.), *New paradigms for college teaching* (pp. 79–102). Interaction.

Cullen, R., & Harris, M. (2009). Assessing learner-centredness through course syllabi. *Assessment and Evaluation in Higher Education, 34(1), 115*–125. https://doi.org/10.1080/02602930801956018

Gannon, K. (2019). How to create a syllabus: Advice guide. *The Chronicle of Higher Education*. https://www.chronicle.com/interactives/advice-syllabus?utm_source=at&utm_medium=en&cid=at

Richmond, A. S., Morgan, R. K., Slattery, J. M., Mitchell, N. G., & Cooper, A. G. (2019). Project Syllabus: An exploratory study of learner-centered syllabi. *Teaching of Psychology, 46*(1), 6–15. https://doi.org/10.1177/0098628318816129

Richmond, A. S., Slattery, J. M., Mitchell, N., Morgan, R. K., & Becknell, J. (2017). Can a learner-centered syllabus change students' perceptions of student-professor rapport and master teacher behaviors? *Scholarship of Teaching and Learning in Psychology, 2*(3), 159–168. https://doi.org/10.1037/stl0000066

Slattery, J. M., & Carlson, J. F. (2005). Preparing an effective syllabus: Current best practices. *College Teaching, 53*(4), 159–164. https://doi.org/10.3200/CTCH.53.4.159-164

Stein, L. (2019). Assessing the value of diversity statements in course syllabi. In J. M. Slattery (Chair), *Project Syllabus: All syllabi can be social justice syllabi.* Symposium at the annual convention of the American Psychological Association, Chicago, IL.

What Role Does Your Syllabus Play?

Maryellen Weimer

I sometimes worry that we don't think about the syllabus as expansively and creatively as we could. We focus, almost exclusively it seems to me, on what should be on it—the information and details it should contain. We do much less thinking about the role of the syllabus—how it can or might function in a course, how it is or could be thought of, and how we do or could make better use of it. So, here's an attempt to broaden our thinking.

Different roles of a syllabus

- **A map:** It lays out the countryside of the course and its content. It may designate the spot where students begin and the place where we hope they'll end. The syllabus is a trip planner, like those old AAA maps that highlighted the best route. A good syllabus tells students—those who pay attention—where they've been, where they are now, and where they're headed. That's a big comfort when the territory is new and unfamiliar.
- **An invitation:** It's an invite to a learning event, and a good syllabus makes it look like a dinner party you wouldn't want to miss. There will be great food and lots of it—that's the course content—stimulating conversation, laughter, learning, and lots of preparing for professional life ahead. Those invited should plan to stay for the whole event. No ducking out early.
- **A contract:** It describes a relationship with obligations. It spells out what students must do and not do, hopefully with more emphasis on the *do*s than on the *don't*s. A good syllabus includes at least a bit of the rationale behind what it obligates students to deliver. Contracts specify what both parties in the relationship will provide. A good syllabus lays out what the teacher will and won't do as well. Usually

contracts are signed, signifying that the terms of the relationship are accepted by both parties.

- **A puzzle, partly assembled:** Every course has lots pieces. The content has been cut up into chunks, modules, and units. The readings are also chopped up and the assignments spread out across the course. On the syllabus, the calendar lists content, exams, and assignments, although it isn't always clear how they fit together. And then there are rules, policies, and prohibitions—things a student should and shouldn't do. Where do these pieces fit in the puzzle? Why are there so many? The syllabus empties the puzzle box, does the initial sorting to locate the edges, and starts putting some of the big pieces together. A well-crafted syllabus guides students as they work to complete the puzzle.
- **A sneak peek:** The syllabus introduces the course and the person teaching it. What's the course about? Does the content look interesting? Is it relevant now or only in the future? Does the teacher seem friendly and approachable? Does it sound like she wants to teach this course? What does he think about students? Does he trust them, like them, and want them to do well? Like a good movie trailer, the syllabus conveys a lot about the course and its instructor. Students read between the lines and form first impressions.
- **An owner's manual:** The teacher who designed this course has prepared a manual that shows how the course operates. The student has purchased the course (quite literally) and now has a manual that explains course specifications. It also makes clear that there are ways to run the course that will cause it to break down, sometimes beyond repair. There's a troubleshooting guide that offers suggestions for what to do when the course isn't running smoothly. It will identify what may be causing the problem and how it might be fixed.

The syllabus doesn't have to be all of these things. It can serve few or many functions. What role does this all-important teaching artifact play in your courses? Think about it; the syllabus is relevant for the entire course. It has everything all in one place—in print and accessible online any time during the course. What promise and potential! Is your syllabus all that it could be in your courses?

Tips for Creating a More Inclusive Syllabus

Ginger R. Fisher and Susan M. Keenan

According to the National Center for Education Statistics' (2019) most recent data, 24 percent of college students are first in their families to attend college (p. 127). First-generation students bring a richness and depth to the student body, but navigating campus as a first-generation student can be arduous. Without the benefit of intergenerational guidance, campus culture can be complicated with barriers that negatively affect persistence and graduation.

The vast majority of campus faculty were not themselves first-generation students and do not respond as helpfully as they might to first-generation students' struggles. The Inclusive Excellence Teacher-Scholar (IE-TS) program at the University of Northern Colorado was created to help faculty understand inequity on our campus, positively shape the experiences of marginalized students, and become agents of change.

When faculty think about equity and inclusive environments, most focus on the classroom and personal interactions with students. And yes, the culture that we create in the classroom is important, but there are other ways that students gain impressions of us as educators.

We invite your reconsideration of the course syllabus and its role in supporting first-generation students. It is often the first point of contact that students have with us, our courses, and the content we hope they will learn. In this article, we share Ginger Fisher's (GF) experience of developing an inclusive syllabus and provide concrete recommendations that have grown out of our professional development (Center for Urban Education, 2018; Dowd & Bensimon, 2015) and become part of our IE-TS program. Our goal is straightforward: to show how the syllabus can become a tool that supports equity and inclusion and at the same still provides all the course details that students need to know.

Viewing your current syllabus

When I (GF) started on the process of making my syllabus more inclusive, I had to take a step back and look at my current syllabus. I felt fairly good about the document. It laid out the course objectives, polices, assignments, grade breakdown, and schedule of topics. I felt like it had all the pieces that I needed, and it had been working well for quite a few years. But when I thought about how it might look to a first-generation student, I realized that there were some problems. The syllabus listed a number of rules and policies along with clearly stated consequences for not following them. It read more like a legal contract than a welcoming invitation to a learning experience. Changes were in order.

Starting with jargon

As in any culture, colleges and universities have their own language, rules, unwritten codes of conduct, and historical practices. The ability to rely on the knowledge of family members who have already navigated these experiences is akin to entering college with a guide and less like traveling solo to a new country where the language and customs are different and unfamiliar. In academia we use language and acronyms that are easy if you know them; we shorten Thursday to R, we list our office hours and think that students know these hours are set aside for them, and we assume that students understand why they're getting a syllabus and how they should use it. Then there are the phrases regularly used on syllabi—"comprehensive exam," "learning objectives," "weighted grade." What those terms mean isn't obvious when you encounter them for the first time. It was clear that I could be more inclusive if I clarified how the course works and what all these terms mean. To do that, I added an overview of what we would be doing each class period and gave a more explicit list of required materials. I also used graphics, color, and formatting to highlight important information. I changed my list of weighted grades to a pie chart so that students could visually see how their work would be assessed. My revised syllabus also showed students the formative, low-stakes assessments in comparison to the summative, higher-stakes assessments.

We also often incorrectly assume that students know to call us "Dr." and not "Mr.," "Mrs.," or "Ms.," so another small but powerful change I made to my syllabus was to let students know my preferred title and pronouns. I also made it clear that I would use their preferred names and pronouns, explaining that I saw this as a way of validating each student's identity. I was surprised at the number of students who commented that this simple addition to the syllabus made them feel welcome and appreciated.

Creating a partnership and validating struggle

I have always viewed my course as a partnership. The students and I work together to reach a set of common goals (the course objectives). But I never made that clear in the syllabus. I started doing so by simply welcoming students to the course. I teach an introductory course taken primarily by first-semester students, and I wanted to acknowledge their achievement of getting into college and pledge my support for their continued success. I do that now at the beginning of my syllabus with a paragraph that congratulates them and shares my excitement at having them in a course that journeys through a topic I love. I close out that introduction with a statement validating their goals and stating my intention to be a resource for students as they make their way through the course. I highlight the partnership by using "we" and "us" rather than "you" or "students." This language makes it clear that we're in an environment that places the students and professor on the same team.

It is critically important to acknowledge that all students struggle at various points in their academic careers and this struggle is a normal part the college experience. Normalizing struggle is especially important for first-generation students, who tend to equate difficulty with a sense of not belonging or an inability to achieve academic goals. To convey this on the syllabus, I devote an entire page to student support. It includes suggestions on how to succeed in the course—what to do before, during, and after a class session—as well as information on getting help. The earlier version of my syllabus simply listed campus resources. Now there's a discussion of each, including what services they provide and how those can be beneficial. I also make sure to point out when a resource is free, something I've stopped assuming every student knows. For some time now, I've used low-stakes homework assignments that allow students to make mistakes. I also drop the lowest exam score. This approach gives students the chance to grow and does not penalize those who might not understand the rigors of college coursework or who have arrived on campus without strong study skills. It also shows that I expect students to hit obstacles during the course.

Welcoming tone and an increased understanding of relevance

Many institutions now require us to list the courses objectives in our syllabus. Historically, I made a list, leaving students to figure out their relevance. Now I list them as course goals and add a description of why each is important and involves skills relevant to future career plans. I hope that makes their value clearer to students.

Often professors <u>underscore words</u> or use **bold** or *italics* to highlight important information on the syllabus. Have you ever considered how students receive that added emphasis? It's often viewed negatively and conveys the idea that students can't figure out for themselves what's important.

It's a good idea to read your syllabus while asking yourself whether it's conveying the positive first impression you intend. I know that mine did not! So I worked to limit "shouting" in the syllabus and to explain policies clearly, collegially, and in a welcoming tone. It's worth noting here that being open and transparent about course policies is especially important for first-generation students. For example, if your syllabus states that no late work will be accepted but in practice you do accept it when there's a valid reason, consider changing the wording on your syllabus. Students used to college culture usually don't hesitate to ask for the extensions, but many first-generation students will not, assuming that the policy in the syllabus stands.

A final word on policies: required institutional policy information—such as (dis)ability or plagiarism statements—cannot always be changed. They cannot be rewritten in language that is welcoming and validating. In these cases, consider providing a preamble that describes the rationale and importance of these institutional policies.

First-generation students often feel immense pressure to do well academically for parents, siblings, and other loved ones who are supporting them personally and financially. The syllabus can be a resource that inclusively supports first-generation students as they pursue their academic goals. I was surprised by how these small changes to my syllabus made a big difference in the support and welcome I now extend to all students.

To see examples of syllabi before and after our IE-TS workshops and for additional resources, visit the University of Northern Colorado's STEM Inclusive Excellence Collective website (https://www.unco.edu/nhs/stem-inclusive-excellence-collective).

References

Center for Urban Education. (2018). *Equity-minded inquiry series: Syllabus Review*. Rossier School of Education, University of Southern California.

Dowd, A. C., & Bensimon, E. M. (2015). Enacting justice as care. In *Engaging the "race question": Accountability and equity in U.S. higher education* (pp. 61–92). Teachers College Press.

National Center for Education Statistics. (2019, January). *Profile of undergraduate students: Attendance, distance and remedial education, degree program and field of study, demographics, financial aid, financial literacy, employment, and military status: 2015–16*. https://nces.ed.gov/pubs2019/2019467.pdf

What Kind of Syllabus?

Maryellen Weimer

A recent study found that professors and students aren't on the same page when it comes to the course syllabus (Lightner & Benander, 2018). How about you and your students? As faculty, we probably don't all see eye to eye, but most of us consider the syllabus a pretty detailed road map that shows students the way through the course. Most of us devote considerable time and energy to developing a syllabus. We write it with the idea that students need to read it, not scan it, even though most of us spend time early in the course carefully going over the syllabus because we've learned the hard way that students don't read it. And most of us politely and patiently respond to any questions students have about the course, even though the syllabus answers most of them. So there are a few issues we might profitably explore.

The study's authors developed four distinct syllabi: a newsletter-style syllabus with interesting graphics; a "promising" syllabus that included detailed rationales for activities and assignments and explained the relationship between assigned readings and the content covered in class; a simple syllabus characterized as direct and concise; and a "warning" syllabus peppered with prohibitions, penalties, and directives. Course content, policies, activities, and assignments were the same across all four. Students and faculty rated each syllabus in terms of its format, what it communicated about the course, and what it communicated about the instructor.

Overall, students had a strong preference for the simple syllabus; faculty, by contrast, preferred the promising syllabus. The warning syllabus didn't get high marks from either group, although I'm still seeing lots of strongly worded statements in syllabi. Further analysis revealed that these faculty and students oriented to the syllabus quite differently. Faculty tended to view it as "a creative work . . . a representation of the effort . . . put into the course" (p. 450). To students, however, the syllabus was a reference document, one they perused for procedural information and consulted as needed.

Underscoring students' perceptions was the amount of time they indicated they'd committed to reading each syllabus: 12 minutes on the promising syllabus (more time than they thought the task merited) compared to eight minutes on each of the other three.

Single studies don't justify broad conclusions, but this one does raise the question of whether we're trying to use syllabi to accomplish unrealistic goals. If students want a concise course reference, maybe that's what we should provide. There's evidence in this study and in other research that the tone of the syllabus does matter. These students didn't respond well to the syllabus full of warnings and consequences. Rather, they wanted a friendly, professional tone and a course taught by a professor who appeared to care. They didn't think it took a lengthy syllabus to get that message across.

Some of us want the syllabus to make students glad they've signed up for the course—if not excited, at least not dreading what's ahead. Could that be conveyed in a note or recorded message to students, one shared electronically or posted on the course website? What about greeting students as they arrive, walking around, shaking a few hands, making some introductions, offering words of welcome, or personally handing out the syllabus?

If we aspire to use the syllabus to communicate something other than concrete course details, we may need to let students know that it contains more, and we've included these additional information for these reasons. What we say about the syllabus needs to be reinforced with actions that illustrate why and how students can use the syllabus as something other than a reference. For example, many of us put learning objectives and the knowledge and skills students can acquire from the course on the syllabus. After a month or so, we could ask students to look at those and check their progress in achieving them.

Maybe teachers and students aren't on the same syllabus page. Maybe we need to turn to another page. Or maybe we should create a new page and see whether we can get students to join us there.

Reference

Lightner, R., & Benander, R. (2018). First impressions: Student and faculty feedback on four styles of syllabi. *International Journal of Teaching and Learning in Higher Education, 30*(3), 443–453. https://files.eric.ed.gov/fulltext/EJ1199421.pdf

The Boring Syllabus

Ed Cunliff

It had happened before, sitting at the computer, working on a syllabus, again, fluctuating between excitement about a new course and a vague sense that life itself was being sucked out of me one sterile byte at a time. I was fighting boredom. And this was supposed to interest students? I tried to imagine it igniting their curiosity, but instead I saw them staring at it with the enthusiasm saved for the fine print on a life insurance policy. But they must read it. It is their life insurance policy for a future full of knowledge and wisdom! It defines how we're going to relate! As I sat there writing my syllabus, I had a vision of the Ferris Bueller video of the professor droning on and on while asking for input: "Anyone? Anyone?" That was not where I wanted to go. I had to stop and rethink what I was doing.

The worst of it

The writing style of the standard syllabus is frequently flat, emotionless, and formulaic. It's made so in part by the list of things that faculty are required to put in the syllabus: contact information, learning objectives, course description, ADA and other policy information, and so on. These policy guidelines are considered necessary for a variety of good reasons. Even so, I have yet to see a policy on syllabi that demands they bore the reader! Much like first impressions of individuals, the course descriptions in the catalog and the syllabus are the "official" first impressions that a student will have of a course. What kind of impressions do they make?

The meta-communication

The concept of meta-communication suggests that the form of the communication, its nonverbal elements, begins to define the teacher-student relationship. So what relationship do I want with my students? What kind of first impression am I interested in making through my syllabus?

I know that students will have some idea of the course based on its title. They will also have an image of a faculty member. They more than likely will project past educational experiences on the course and expect what they have experienced to continue. They don't arrive in my course as blank slates.

I want to inspire curiosity about my field. I'm passionate about it and want them to see that passion. I'm also a lifelong learner and don't want to hide that either. In fact, I'd like to encourage students to join me on that journey so that we can learn from each other. Hopefully, they will know immediately that this is a unique course and that their participation will help make it so. I'd like them to see the immediate relevance of the course and get a sense that their perspectives and experiences matter. Those are the messages I want to convey in the syllabus, and here are some of the ways I've tried communicating them. It's still a work in progress.

Succinctly stated strategic syllabi suggestions

I start by trying to get their attention visually. If everyone else is using Times Roman 12 font, I use something different. It still has to be readable, but many of those other font options are. I include a picture of myself, usually a candid shot and a couple-of-sentences-long biography. I tend to go the route of my passion for the field, but I consider identifying favorite hobbies equally appropriate.

Sometimes I add photos of prominent individuals in the field. I usually include a photo or two of students interacting (no faces for identification) as a means of telling them that we will be actively engaging each other. Quotes (again I like those by notables in the field) are another way to add interest and pique curiosity. I can see using a quote from a student offering some reaction or assessment of the course—a kind of endorsement message.

Why not a question or two on the first page? What do you already know about (class title)? What do you hope to learn about . . . ? How will you use . . . ? The use of questions cues students that there will be interaction and that they are expected to engage. It also tells them that questions are OK. Students should be asking them.

Actions, including those taken by students, have consequences. I go to pains to phrase them positively. Some do threaten students with the loss of points for various behaviors, but I try to support students. Class participation is a positive, for instance. Research documents that engagement promotes learning, and I assume that students want to learn. I am trying to set a climate that tells them this is a positive journey, and we are taking the trip together. Wherever possible I will use the word "we," hoping to open the door for collaborative learning, with me as learner as well as their instructor.

In the end

I'm not proposing that we make our syllabi into marketing materials. We need to describe course content accurately. We need to include the necessary policies. It is about balance and recognizing the meta messages the syllabus conveys about the course. It's our first attempt to establish those relationships with students that promote learning. My goal: I'm working to create a syllabus that puts life into the subject!

Classroom Climate and the Syllabus

Maryellen Weimer

Classroom climate "profoundly shapes" the experience of both instructor and students. That's a claim made by two authors of a study that looked at syllabi from sociology courses to see what they said about classroom climate (Valentin & Grauerholz, 2019, p. 219). They found that most of the statements focused on students and their need to respect each other. Students are key, but they don't provide the leadership needed to establish or maintain the classroom climate. That's a teacher's responsibility.

Does putting a statement in the syllabus about the desired climate help to create it? In this review the authors looked at almost 900 syllabi. Only one in five contained some sort of statement on climate. That could mean a big chunk of faculty don't think climate is important enough to mention, or maybe those folks don't think a statement in the syllabus does anything to create the climate, which is especially true when students don't read the syllabus. But then, if teachers suspect students aren't reading the syllabus, they usually talk about everything it contains. Syllabus and teacher statements can help create a climate for learning in a course, but I firmly believe the classroom climate gets established by the behavior inside it. If a teacher claims to value divergent opinions but then argues vehemently when a student states such an opinion, that action says far more about the climate than what the teacher has said or written.

The authors' analysis of 100 syllabus statements in this study uncovered four common ways these sociology faculty conceptualized classroom climate. First and foremost they understood it as students' respecting each other. Seventy-nine of the descriptions included statements to that effect. Between one-fifth and one-fourth of the statements referred to creating a safe space in the classroom, to scholarly engagement (i.e., keeping the conversation professional and not personal), and to accepting individual responsibility (which usually had to do with students coming to class prepared).

It's interesting how frequently those of us in higher education use metaphors to describe classroom climate, starting with the term itself. What does it refer to in a course? Is the idea of creating a "safe" space any clearer? It isn't that the referent is a space free from physical danger. The authors describe "shaping [a] classroom's interactional and socio-emotional landscape" (p. 220). Are these descriptors that make sense to students? To teachers?

Some very early work on classroom climate (see, for instance, Fraser, 1986) assumed it evolved from sets of relationships—between the teacher and the class as a whole; the teacher and individual students, especially as they interact in front of others in the class; and between the students as they relate individually or in groups. Those various relationships become the context within which respect does or doesn't occur. Respect isn't the "climate" but an example of an action in a "good" one. Because it's a course, that context creates expectations that the relationship will be professional, not personal. Teachers and students can be friendly toward one another, but theirs are not peer friendships.

The new insight for me in this research was that opener: the climate in a course profoundly shapes both instructor and student experience. Haven't we all had a course in which the students connected and behaved in ways that made it a wonderful or horrible experience for us? Our relationship with the class gelled or turned sour. Teaching can be heaven or it can be hell. Fortunately, having it mostly somewhere in between keeps us grounded and sane.

But the effect the climate has on all of us means it's a shared responsibility. The respect a good climate requires isn't just respect between students. It's the respect they need to show us and equally importantly the respect we must show them. When it comes to creating the climate, students look to us for leadership. We can't create it without them, but we can lead the way. A climate will be defined with or without our involvement. Without us that pretty much guarantees less than optimal learning conditions for the course.

References

Fraser, B. J. (1986). *Classroom environment.* Croom Helm.

Valentin J., & Grauerholz, L. (2019). Exploring classroom climate in sociology courses using syllabi. *Teaching Sociology, 47*(3), 219–230. https://doi.org/10.1177/0092055X19850252

Special Considerations When Drafting an Online Course Syllabus

Wren Mills

The first time I taught fully online, I assumed that, apart from the attendance policy, the syllabus from my hybrid class would work perfectly well for the new class. I realized quickly that this was not the case. There are several elements that need to be added to a syllabus when teaching an online course.

Outside obligations

The first thing to remember is that online students can be quite different from those who come to campus. They are likely to vary in age, experience (both in the classroom and in the workplace), and confidence. They might be caring for ailing partners or parents, raising children, or working full time—perhaps all the above. Some students might be active duty military and deployed overseas.

As a result, there will likely be times when you need to provide more leeway for students to work their studies around other obligations. This does not mean relaxing your grading standards, but rather having a willingness to make accommodations for students who have conflicts. If a student shows the responsibility to come forward with a conflict as soon as they know about it, I will work with that student to provide extra time or whatever is needed to get around the conflict. For example, I allow students to submit work up to one week past its deadline for a 10 percent deduction in the grade and no other extensions. This allows for those times when "life happens" and might help an otherwise excellent student from losing a significant number of points.

Connection

Because of the distance between instructor and classmates, online students are more likely to feel disconnected from you and their peers. To help make connections, an instructor can require students to post an introductory bio via blog or discussion. The instructor should also seed the discussion with their own bio or an introductory paragraph at the start of your syllabus. The bio should be something of interest, not just a list of credentials. For example, I share that I met my English husband online in 1997 as I was preparing for a semester at Cambridge. I also let students know that I have not just cats and dogs, but pet chickens, too. Details like these humanize you and help students connect with you from the very beginning.

Communication

We need to encourage our online students to reach out to us when they need help, knowing that they don't have the benefit of asking questions before, during, or after a class. Information that includes how and when to communicate with the instructor needs to be front and center on the syllabus. Also, many online faculty think they do not need to establish set office hours, because students can always make appointments. But this is a mistake. Establishing online office hours that students can "drop in" for demonstrates that you are approachable and invites interactions more than simply telling them that they can make appointments to meet with you.

Sometimes, however, student questions are better answered by campus offices. While on-campus students generally know about these offices and where to find them, online students may not. For this reason, an online syllabus needs to carry more information about support services for students, such as the writing center. Many schools have developed a "one-stop shop" student portal, such as WKU's Student Resource Portal (https://www.wku.edu/online/srp), to let students know that campus services are at their fingertips. This can help them get the support they need and feel more connected to your campus, which improves retention.

More information

Because online faculty do not have the luxury to elaborate on points that they cover in their syllabi, they need to go into more go into detail in an online syllabus than a face-to-face syllabus. If you are fond of adding helpful hints when going over your syllabus in a face-to-face class, such as the need to reserve a time with the writing center at least a week out before the end of the semester, when there is a rush, then you will need to add them to the online version of the syllabus.

There is also some unique information that an online class syllabus needs to include. For instance, a commonly overlooked item is the time zone the instructor is in. It is also important to establish the time zone the class will use for any live events. Generally, this is the time zone of the host university.

It is also important that you craft your contact or communication policy carefully. Studies show that students feel satisfied with response times within 48 hours, but consider that if they are getting in touch, that likely means they are stuck and aren't able to progress in their work. A two-day delay is a lot! My personal policy is to promise a returned email within 24 hours unless I am ill or without connectivity, and this seems to work well. On weekends, I let them know they will have an answer by noon. During the week, they know I have my email on all day and to normally expect a quick response. Students learn to take advantage of this, and so I seldom get emails on the weekends. The important thing is that students know how you prefer to be contacted and how quickly to expect a response. Make sure the policy you write is one you are comfortable with and can stick to.

Additionally, as odd as it may seem, telling students they will need their own computers is another important policy. Even today, students try to borrow computers from neighbors or family members or think they can do their coursework exclusively on their smartphones. Some even go to a local library to use the computers there, despite the short time restrictions.

I also make sure the students know not to panic if they submit the wrong file or something odd happens with the LMS. They can just email me the correct file or let me know if I need to reset something. Sharing specifically what file formats you accept is also helpful for adult learners, especially if you prefer something other than a standard Word file (be sure to share how to convert to that format too). Many online learners feel like they will be penalized for these common errors. Letting them know up front how to handle these issues eases their minds and prevents panicked emails and calls.

Another policy to consider is an inclement weather policy. In my area, we can have ice storms that knock out power for days, if not weeks. I've recently had distance students caught up in hurricanes, typhoons, extreme flooding, and tornadoes. What will you do if your students are affected by those kinds of events? Having a policy in place now means having one less thing to worry about should they occur.

The important thing to remember is that online students are not likely to have the same characteristics as in-person students, just as your online course will not work in the same way as your in-person offering. Because of this, spending time considering each policy when crafting your online syllabus will pay off in the long run.

Part 4
Planning Assignments and Assessments

Could Your Assignments Use a Tune-Up?

Maryellen Weimer

How do students think about assignments? A lot never get past the idea that they're basically unpleasant things faculty make them do. What does interest a lot of students is finding out what the teacher wants in the assignment—not so much what the assignment asks but more what the teacher "likes." Discover that and there's a better chance of a good grade, or so the thinking goes. Unfortunately, very few students look at an assignment and think, "Now there's an interesting learning opportunity."

And how do faculty think about assignments? With multiple courses and lots of other work besides, with each new assignment developed there's a tendency to first consider the amount of grading that will come with it. And then there's how to deal with assignments that come in late or not at all, assignments that may not have been completed by the students who turned them in, assignments that don't merit a passing mark—all potential headaches for the teacher.

I have two other concerns about assignments:

1. The extent to which they are recycled, used again semester after semester
2. The extent to which the same or very similar assignments are widely used across course levels and disciplines

This collection of issues and concerns makes this piece a gentle reminder of how significantly assignments shape what and how students learn in a course. An assignment has the potential to promote learning on three fronts. First (and some would say most importantly), **assignments promote content learning**. An assignment can't be done well (or even not so well) without getting up close and personal with the content. That being the case, it's necessary for faculty to regularly revisit an assignment in terms of what content students will encounter as they complete it. Is it important content? Interesting content? Challenging content? Content that illustrates organizing principles or central concepts? How does the assignment advance what students should know by the end of the course?

Second, **assignments promote the development of skills**, usually skills associated with learning and skills that can be used across a lifetime. So what skills does doing the assignment develop? Here there's a tendency for faculty to be more idealistic than pragmatic. We want students to develop all kinds of complex skills: critical thinking, problem-solving, organization, integration, questioning, in-depth analysis, and reading and writing skills. Yes, these are important skills, and there's nothing wrong with high standards for students, but our thinking about assignments needs to be less all-inclusive and more specific. The questions we need to ask are these: What skills is the content in this course well-positioned to develop? And then, with a critical eye on the assignment, what skills (maybe it's just one skill) is this assignment in a good position to advance? This is especially important when students have multiple skills they need to remediate. Skills are best developed one at a time, with fixed and focused attention, accompanied with deliberate practice. So targeting skills in a course and in the course's assignments aids their development. It's better than a generic commitment to comprehensive skill development.

And finally, **assignments can enlarge the student's understanding** of their development as a learner. But most students aren't going to reflect on their skills without prompting, especially those who aren't paying much attention to learning in general. I don't ever remember thinking about how I was learning when I in college, even in grad school. The questions for students can be about the process: How much time did you think the assignment would take to complete? Did you over- or underestimate? Did you collaborate with others? Was that helpful? What was the hardest part of the assignment? The easiest part? Did the assignment call for skills you need to further develop? If motivation was a problem, how did you get yourself to work on the assignment? Questions like these lead to what should be asked after every assignment: What did you learn about yourself as a learner?

Assignments are what students ride on their way to learning. Our responsibility is to provide good vehicle maintenance and recognition when it's time for a trade-in.

Assignments Don't Just Happen

Deborah Bracke

I often wonder what students think about the assignments we create. In my experience, they frequently see assignments as having a limited and somewhat task-oriented relationship with their course work. Their concern about what counts for a grade is frequently one-dimensional and often usurps the lasting values and capacities I hope to develop. This frustrates me, and I imagine it frustrates other teachers as well.

How can we convince our students that assignments don't just "happen"—that curricular decisions are not based on expediency but involve careful planning, intentionality, and time? How can we connect our students to the professional decisions we've made *before* we even hand out the assignment?

Looking at the literature, I knew there were extensive studies that established the value of active, engaged, and collaborative ways of learning for students in higher education. I also understood that a common thread throughout this established research base was an emphasis on critical inquiry and shared experiences. (I know this is nothing new to those with a strong commitment to the academic community. In many respects the intellectual roots of critical inquiry and collaborative learning are traceable to Socrates.) But my more recent notions of intentionality were heightened when I revisited the works of Dewey, who alluded to the power of the latent curriculum and Vygotsky, who stated that learning is a social and collaborative act.

Might there be a way to use this evidence base to invite students to look more closely at our own pedagogical practices? Might there be a way to develop assessments that encourage students to not only "complete the assignment" but also reflect and think responsibly about the choices they've made—and ask, "Why would a teacher have me do an assignment like this?" How might we convince our students that our purpose goes beyond graduation requirements, program retention, and evidence collection?

I had an idea.

To get my students to think more critically about the professional decisions I made in creating a purposeful assessment, I introduced "cover sheets" as a course requirement for many of our class assignments. I explained that there were a multitude of ways I could ask them to demonstrate their understanding. What were my hopes and strategies in devising this particular assignment?

I asked them to reflect and write a response to the following:

> Good curricular decisions are not based on expediency. Classroom instruction involves careful planning and teachers must make prudent decisions about what they will teach and how they will teach it. Why do you think I developed *this particular assignment* to provide evidence of an EDUC 340 learning target?

Since many of our assignments are completed collaboratively, these cover pages advanced the ideas embraced by Dewey and Vygotsky. For example, in our first assignment for EDUC 340 (Methods of Inclusion), students were asked to skim the 79 pages of 105 ILCS 5/Article 14 of the Illinois School Code and to write a cogent summary statement (52 words or fewer) that explained how this legislation relates to students with disabilities. When students asked, "Why 52 words?," I informed them that although the Preamble to the United States Constitution is only 52 words, it is considered by many to be the most important political instrument of modern times.

I challenged them to emulate this brevity.

My own rationale for this assignment was twofold. First, I wanted to introduce our teacher candidates to Article 14 of the Illinois School Code, a series of statutes that address the education of students with disabilities and other special needs. Second, it was important for me to reinforce the value our department places on distilling main ideas with precision and clarity.

Students appeared to complete the assignment without much difficulty and shared their 52-word summary statements in groups of four. They turned in their cover pages separately. Responses to "Why do you think I created this particular assignment?" (which did not require a word count) were quite varied.

Student A displayed a rudimentary understanding of the rationale suggested: "I think you wanted us to learn about certain disabilities, how to teach students with special needs, and how to write goals for our students."

Student B demonstrated a more accurate understanding of my rationale proposed that the purpose of the assignment was to

> broaden our sense of what students with disabilities are able to *achieve* with the appropriate supports and services. You wanted us to engage in the writing process and to concisely identify main ideas because that is what will be necessary when we write IEP goals that are specific to the needs of a certain disability and are based on what a student can do. I think you wanted us to begin to think as a teacher might have to in relation to the legalities of the IEP and referral process. Since you wanted us to share our ideas within our groups, you also wanted us to begin to build strong, supportive relationships in class.

Student C offered reasons somewhat disarrayed. Here's an excerpt:

> I think that you wanted us to write concisely so that we can be more effective and efficient in in the classroom—and to encourage our arguments to have more impact and be stronger and less vague. I also think you wanted us to learn the proper format for the cover page. It's important to know the format of assignments. You wanted us to understand that we must follow the laws that have been written. I also learned that even though the Preamble to the Constitution has just 52 words, it provides an introduction to the laws we still follow today—almost 250 years later. So, we should be able to convey important thoughts in 52 words too!

It's interesting to note how differently my students perceived and dissected the content assigned to them. Student A assumed a simplicity that doesn't exist, Student B was fairly spot on, and Student C offered a shallow, rambling answer that had little bearing on the assignment's intent. But regardless of their reflections, I liked the fact that my students were able to think more broadly about their assignment.

As I plan for next semester, I will continue to use these cover pages (at least every now and then). In some respects, they offer me a chance to converse with students on a more individual basis. Students are invited *inside* the assignment and challenged to think through the personal and professional beliefs that determine what is worth knowing. This is a space between content and pedagogy that can not only strengthen the student-teacher relationship but also empower students to regard assessment as a process rather than a single event. In this way, completing assignments is viewed not as an ending point but as a seamless learning experience.

The use of cover sheets also tempers the sender–receiver hierarchy students often encounter in the college classroom. They encourage students to be more active participants in the process of learning and provide us, as professors, with an opportunity to reflect on whether a given assessment is the best way to optimize student learning. When we consider students' understandings more intimately, we can use these evaluative or emotive impressions to design or improve assignments in any content area.

Regardless of discipline, assignments don't just happen. The assessments we create are deliberate, planned, and secured in a curriculum with students' best interests in mind. I believe our students can reach a level of understanding that is above and beyond the subject matter if we ask the simple question *why*.

Designing Homework That Enhances Learning

Maryellen Weimer

What kind of homework assignments promote learning? We don't need research to confirm that doing homework benefits most (maybe it's all) college students. But there are some vexing issues. If the homework is graded and those grades count, students will do the homework. But then all that homework must be graded. That can involve a huge time investment for the teacher. So faculty respond by designing homework assignments that can be graded quickly or aren't graded at all, with students getting credit for completing them, provided the work shows they've made a reasonable effort. Both of those options tend to compromise the amount of learning that results from doing the homework assignment.

A faculty research team tested an interesting homework design feature in multiple sections of an undergraduate educational psychology course (Galyon et al., 2015). Homework was assigned in every class session, and it consisted of 10 to 12 short-answer essay questions. Even though most of the questions could be answered in two to five sentences, that's enough homework grading to bury most teachers. In one of the experimental conditions, students simply got credit for the percentage of questions answered in each homework assignment—the completion option. In the other, answers to 10 percent of the questions (randomly selected) were graded according to a quality criterion explained in the article. In this option students knew some of their answers would be graded, they just didn't know which answers. The second approach reduced the instructor's grading time by 90 percent. Credit for both assignment options was the same.

Researchers were interested in two questions. "The first goal of the study was to determine if a randomized credit contingency [the second option] would produce higher-quality answers than assessment of all homework items for completion" (p. 65). "The second goal was to see if improvement in the quality of students' homework would indirectly improve their exam performance" (p. 65). And the results confirmed both of these hoped-for conclusions. "Setting randomized reward contingencies specifically for accuracy of homework produced both significantly higher accuracy and length of homework answers than a reward contingency based on completion of the homework" (p. 73). The randomized answer option was also associated "with modest but significant gains in adjusted exam scores" (p. 73).

In a discussion of how these findings relate to other research, the study's authors note that over the past decade, research has identified a number of factors that either contribute to or actually predict exam scores. They list (and reference) homework completion, critical-thinking ability, participation in class discussion, generic vocabulary, and student efficacy. "None of these studies considered separately constitute a dramatic contribution to exam scores, but taken together they provide a relatively extensive picture of what accounts for exam performance" (p. 74).

Completing a homework assignment like this one not only promotes the learning of course content, but it also brings students to class prepared to talk about the content. They can answer questions and add insights, and that makes for richer class discussions.

Design details, even small ones, do make a difference. In this case they encouraged students to prepare longer and more accurate answers to questions about course material, and those answers were associated with better exam scores. And by reducing the number of answers that were graded, this design detail makes giving regular and substantial homework assignments a viable option for faculty members. Would students object to having to prepare answers for which they got no credit? In this case, exam questions were conceptually linked to the homework assignment questions. An example in the article illustrates this connection. If students are shown the relationship between homework questions and those on the exam, that may dampen their objections.

Reference

Galyon, C. E., Voils, K. L., Blondin, D. A., & Williams, R. L. (2015). The effect of randomized homework contingencies on college students' daily homework and unit exam performance. *Innovative Higher Education, 40*(1), 63–77. https://doi.org/10.1007/s10755-014-9296-1

Teaching the How: Three Ways to Support Failure

Paul Hanstedt

I give students in my literature courses a lot of weird assignments: I have them make and post films about why people should read Dickens. I tell them these films should show careful analysis of the text but should also entertain and have good music so that viewers won't get bored. I ask students in my gen ed capstone to create campaigns advocating for the liberal arts. I make my creative writing students create a job portfolio unrelated to their professional aspirations as writers. They object: They want to write stories. Why in the world should they articulate a set of conceptual skills they'd bring to a State Department position?

I do this because I want to shake my students out of the transactional malaise that is most academic writing. As Arum and Roksa pointed out in 2011, most students assume that professors assign papers because that's what professors are supposed to do—not because these papers have any relation to real learning. Students see most paper assignments as meaningless. I think these weird assignments grab their attention and make it more likely that they'll understand that there's something here that really matters.

I also use nontraditional assignments because they require more deliberate thought on the part of students. Most good students will tell me, in moments of weakness or bravado, that they can crank out an A paper in a night—indeed, they've done so many times. I want to prevent that. Something done with that little time-on-task likely won't lead to much real learning. The fundamental purpose of any assignment should be the forward movement of learning.

And there's one added bonus to assigning something other than the ordinary: it forces *me* to be more deliberate. If I'm going to ask students to create a game that teaches players about the power of the humanities or design a poster that conveys the complexities of a social-epistemic approach to teaching writing, I know that the classroom is going to be anything but business as usual. Yes, we still cover content; students will learn the basics and then some. But the questions I ask during discussion change, the types of connections students are making on their own change, the directions lectures, dialogues and debates go becomes more unpredictable. With assignments like these I can't just send students off to do their thing; I have to *teach.* I have to think carefully about what I'm doing in the classroom.

All of which is a roundabout way of saying this: sometimes as teachers, I think we're so concerned with covering course content that we forget to think about the bigger picture: why the content matters, how students use it, explore it, contextualize it, practice skills related to it, and make sense out of it.

And the thing is? That stuff—the contextualizing and making sense? That's HARD.

What's more, if we follow traditional models that deliver content for 13 weeks and end with a huge project but never give students the opportunity to practice the skills necessary for that assignment, then we've got an ethical issue. Because the really clever students who learn quickly and have support networks will be fine. And the rest . . . will not. And if we take seriously our role as *educators* but only the already high-performing students get As, then we're not doing a very good job.

Content matters. Don't get me wrong. Students need strong content in order to succeed on a project *and* to succeed in life. But we also need to give students time to work with that content, to experiment with it, fail with it, to try again, to get a little better, to start gaining a sense of their capabilities, and to take on a harder problem. And then a harder problem. And then begin to achieve some level of mastery.

In the end, I'm going to argue that the key component in education is making room for failure. On the most basic level, this means making space in the course syllabus for feedback and revisions of not just early drafts of written work, but oral presentations, digital projects, quantitative projects, and scientific posters. The go-to term these days for something like this is "scaffolding," but like a lot of go-to language in academia, it's hard to figure out exactly what that means. So I'm going to simplify and propose that faculty explore and implement a series of small focused practice sessions that are *ungraded, minimally graded,* or *proportionally graded.*

Those terms are perhaps self-explanatory, but allow me to unpack them nevertheless.

Ungraded refers to assignments or student work that doesn't get any grade at all (surprise!). Think, for instance, about that physics equation students to graph in groups. Or that impromptu speech students give as a precursor to their major presentation. Or that image or concept map they create to illustrate a complex theory that may perplex their peers. Think also about smaller out-of-class assignments: finding a single really good source on a topic for class discussion the next day; attempting to apply a sociological theory to a family dynamic; analyzing a mainstream media article that references the content being learned in the chemistry course. My colleague Hannah Robbins, who teaches mathematics, has the students in her courses design the rubrics for their major projects. The rubrics themselves are ungraded, and while the work students do creating them doesn't directly prepare them for the final oral presentations (or papers, or posters), they come away from this work with an insider's understanding of what's expected of them in the larger project. So, *ungraded*, but *invaluable*.

Minimally graded can refer to two types of student work. The first are relatively small assignments that students prepare out of class for which they receive an individual grade. Such an assignment might be, for instance, a simple case study students work on in preparation for a more complex case study later in the course or on an exam. My colleague Jen Jackl, in communications, has students design an activity illustrating for the rest of the class a complex social interaction or concept. Engineering students could be asked to come up with three reasonable, feasible solutions for a problem, then lead a class discussion on which is best and why.

The grade for this initial run should be no more than 5 percent of the overall final grade for the course. Indeed, it may be even smaller: I've seen accounting and statistics professors assign a series of series of practice runs each worth 1.5 percent of the overall grade as a precursor to more complicated projects. The key here is that (a) the work has to model key skills necessary for success later in the term, (b) the grade has to be small enough that students falling flat on their faces won't prevent overall success in the course, and (c) students have time to do the work *outside of class*. With the exception of exams, very little work done in the classroom should receive a grade, even a small one.

The second version of minimally graded work has less to do with the overall weight of the work toward the final grade than with the level of effort required of the instructor. An example of this comes from Heidi Hanrahan, an award-winning English professor at Shepherd University in West Virginia. Every day—or every other day, or twice a week, or whatever keeps students on track but doesn't overwhelm you—students show up with a typed response to the day's reading. This response should consist of a quote that serves as an epigraph—a line or two that students really love, or really hate, or that really confuses them. The rest of the page should be a thoughtful unpacking of this quotation, exploring and complicating the liking, the disagreeing, or the confusion.

The purpose of an assignment like this is for students to explore their own thinking about a text while polishing their analytical writing skills. As such, the *grade* is really kind of secondary: the assignment isn't intended to be formal or even perfectly grammatical—simply having students engage in messy, sometimes contradictory, always critically exploratory writing is enough. As a result, when I adopt this assignment in my own classes, I simply give students a checkmark if they've taken the process seriously enough. I also make the occasional comment, but usually in a conversational, nonjudgmental kind of way. I call this "white wine grading," for reasons that are perhaps obvious.

That said, though these are minimally graded on my part, they *do* count for 15 percent of the overall course grade. Students who get checks on 90 percent or more receive an A for that portion of the grade; students who get checks for 80–89 percent receive a B; 70–79 percent merits a C. Students who do less than 70 percent fail the entire class, because, ungraded or not, conversational or not, these assignments *matter*, the kinds of learning that occur as students write and think and unpack are crucial to their development. I wouldn't ask them to do it if that weren't the case.

The third type of response, *proportionally graded,* is relatively simple: students engage in an increasingly complex set of preliminary assignments that prepare them for a summative project. The earliest, easiest versions of this preliminary work count for very little (say, 5–10 percent of the overall grade); the middle versions count for more (10–15 percent); and the final versions count for a great deal (25 percent or more). So, for instance, early in his geoscience course my colleague Chris will give his students rock samples that are relatively easy to analyze in terms of making drilling recommendations; later he'll give them more complicated samples, with more "noise"—that is, meaningless data—and less-clear recommendations; and at the end of the course he'll provide students with complex and messy samples where they'll essentially have to construct conclusions on their own. The early case studies will count for 10 percent of the final grade, the middle ones for 15 percent, and the final one for between 20 and 25 percent.

An approach like this could, of course, be applied in nearly every field: sociology or psychology students might examine increasingly complex case studies; literature or history students might explore more and more complicated texts or artifacts. In the end, this approach—this scaffolding or whatever you want to call it—seems *obvious*, right?

But then . . . how come we don't do it this more often? How come we don't include assignments like these into our syllabi, and set aside time for them during the semester?

Because we feel pressure to cover content. Because we've been persuaded that teaching these skills is not our job. Because we forget how acclimated we are to the work of our fields, how much of it we take as a given, as "normal"—even when it's not. Because we forget how often we ourselves failed and how much we learned when we did.

And when we forget that, then . . . well, I worry that we've failed again. And not in a good way.

Reenvisioning Rubrics: A Few Brief Suggestions

Perry Shaw

Linda Suskie's *Assessing Student Learning* documents a wide variety of common assessment errors. They result from the subjective nature of grades in all but the most factual subjects. Many failures point to the need for more objectivity and a better system of accountability, including leniency, generosity, and severity errors; halo, contamination, similar-to-me, and first-impression biases; and that most common of errors, rater drift—that is, the unintentional redefining of scoring criteria as the marker grows tired.

There is no perfect solution to the challenges of meaningful grading, but many of us have found that rubrics help move us toward greater objectivity. They do so by breaking the desired outcomes into individual elements. However, when rubrics rely on general terms like *excellent*, *good*, *fair*, and *poor*, they can still be highly subjective. Those terms encourage instructors merely to get a general "feel" for a student's work and, based on this initial impression, subconsciously (or consciously) assess accordingly across items in the rubric. More detailed descriptions of these terms can improve outcomes, but those explanations can become rigid and confusing.

Here are some suggestions which, although still not perfect, have been helpful for me and my colleagues at my institution. They are approaches that also help my students better understand what instructors need from them. After applying these suggestions, I find that students don't repeat the same mistakes as often as they did when I used more generic terms on my rubrics.

1. Replace evaluative headings with more descriptive terms: for example, "clearly evident," "evident but in need of some development," "evident but in need of a lot of development," and "not evident." It is difficult to entirely remove the subjective element from qualitative assessment, but I have found that students understand these

descriptors better than more evaluative headings.

2. Use the headings "extensive treatment," "moderate treatment," and "no treatment" when the assignment focuses on a dialogue between theory and practice. For example, when looking at the cultural and social factors that influence a specific case study, there are multiple areas in which a student might engage with the theory; it is not necessary to address every area in every case. Assessment should rest on the areas selected and the balance between the areas addressed. There's more subjectivity involved here, so I don't regularly use terms such as these.
3. Provide the rubric in advance. I know there is significant debate on this point; some decry the possibility of undermining creativity and initiation if students approach the rubric in a rigid and mechanistic fashion. However, since I began providing the rubric up front, student complaints about assessments have dramatically declined. Many students have found the rubrics helpful guidelines that develop their critical writing skills.
4. Include a comments section following the rubric table and provide more positive than negative comments. Students are more willing to look at areas in need of improvement if they sense they have made progress on the journey. As a basic rule of thumb, I have found that my students can only cope with a maximum of three negative comments on their work. If students are flooded with too many suggestions, they end up ignoring them all.
5. Find positive ways to give a negative critique. For example, "The next time you do work like this I would urge you to consider the following . . ."
6. Don't place a grade anywhere on the paper or the rubric. My experience has been that the moment students see the grade, that's all they think about. They pay more attention to the grade than to the feedback you've provided. We have to give grades eventually, but if we can delay this, then there is a better chance that students will focus on the feedback.
7. Have students self-assess using the rubric. The ability to make judgments about your own work is an essential metacognitive skill. With practice, student self-assessment skills can grow. This also has the side benefit of letting you know the extent to which you have adequately taught not merely the content of the course but also the methodological elements. For example, through a student self-assessment you are able to see whether they are able to judge whether

they have clearly stated their thesis or provided a critical reflection on differing perspectives of an issue.

8. Require students to respond to your assessment of their work, describing ways in which they might do similar work differently in future. You could do this before giving them the final grade. One of our faculty members includes student responses to the assessment as 10 percent of the final course grade. Approaches like this encourage a detailed reading of the comments you've provided.

Rubrics aren't perfect, but they help; at least, they have in my experience. They make it easier for me to accomplish the key purpose of assessment, which is learning. Any tool we use should be designed so that it strengthens the quality of students' learning.

The Value of Rubrics for Teachers

Maryellen Weimer

Rubrics clarify assignment details for students. They provide an operational answer to the frequently asked student question, "What do you want in this assignment?" They make grading more transparent and can be used to help students develop those all-important self-assessment skills. For teachers, rubrics expedite grading and can make it a more objective process.

But there's another benefit for teachers that's not often mentioned, and that's the power of rubrics to clarify thinking about the knowledge and skills the teacher wants to assess. Teachers do a great deal of assessment, across multiple courses, semester after semester. It's easy for the response to student work to become habitual, automatic, and not always thoughtful. After grading so many hundreds of essays and short answers, the good, the bad, and the ugly are easy to pick out.

The process of creating a rubric forces close consideration of whatever is being assessed—its component parts, features, or characteristics. It also promotes clearer understanding of what a performance or product looks like when it's not right, only partly accomplished, good enough as it is, or everything it ought to be. With rubrics, teachers can not only quickly identify different quality levels, they know why an essay or answer belongs in that category.

Rubrics can be simple or detailed to the nth degree, but they don't have to be complex to be beneficial. Here's an example that illustrates a discussion-group rubric used by a history teacher in an online course (Stern, 2015). She writes that she adapted it from another source. Here are two of the four categories on the rubric.

A or A–: Timely discussion contributions. Comments are meaningful and show preparedness, reflecting course readings. In-depth thought and contributions add to the overall learning of the other individuals in the course. Demonstration of courtesy and respect to others.

C+ to C–: Overall contributions are not meaningful—and include types of comments such as "*good idea*" or "*I agree.*" Very little evidence of having read course materials or giving any in-depth thought to the reading. Failure to participate in at least two discussions during the posting period. (p. 487)

Rubrics can be beneficial in any aspect of instruction—an in-class activity, a major assignment, a teacher's quizzing strategy, a course, and probably most beneficial of all, the levels of learning resulting from a sequence of courses or a whole major or program.

Here's a second example. A group of chemists worked with teaching staff to develop an assessment strategy that would help them understand "the extent to which students were able to think critically about or solve laboratory-based problems across the curriculum, with particular attention to the application of chemical instrumentation" (Shadle et al., 2012, p. 319). They opted to develop a rubric because "cognitive skills, such as critical thinking or problem solving are difficult to measure with a conventional 'test,' graded for correct vs. incorrect answers" (p. 319). Their rubric is anchored around these three criteria:

1. It identifies the important or relevant features of the problem.
2. In formulating a strategy for the solution of the problem, the student presents a complete justification or explanation for the strategy.
3. It provides an effective strategy that is likely to work to solve the chemical problem.

For each criterion, emerging, developing, and mastering levels are described.

Teachers can create rubrics alone and achieve the benefits described here, but chances are good those benefits will be achieved on a much bigger scale if developing the rubric is a collaborative process. Say a group of teachers in a department or program aspire to develop students' critical-thinking skills. What are the identifying features of those skills? At what different levels might they occur on the way to full development? Even if those teachers don't end up agreeing on all parts of the rubric, the conversation will likely have been a rich learning experience for all involved. And if a rubric is mutually acceptable, then teachers with a shared goal are working from the same playbook.

References

Shadle, S. E., Brown, E. C., Towns, M. H., & Warner, D. L. (2012). A rubric for assessing students' experimental problem-solving ability. *Journal of Chemical Education, 89*(3), 319–325. https://doi.org/10.1021/ed2000704

Stern, A. (2015). Bridging the gap: Replicating the interactivity of the physical classroom in an online environment. *The History Teacher, 48*(3), 483–504. http://www.societyforhistoryeducation.org/pdfs/M15_Stern.pdf

Using Specifications Grading to Deepen Student Thinking

Flower Darby

Do you use auto-graded multiple-choice and true-false quizzes and exams? If so, why?

Is it because you're convinced that these forms of assessment are rigorous and authentic instruments for measuring student learning? Or is it because, given that you are teaching larger enrollment classes with fewer resources and support, you don't know what else to do?

It's the latter for many of my faculty colleagues when I ask about their use of an LMS or publisher auto-graded tests. They simply don't know what else to do.

But I think most of us would agree that these forms of assessment can be problematic. Often, multiple-choice quizzes don't measure higher-order cognition, such as problem-solving, analysis, synthesis, or academic writing. Don't get me wrong: auto-graded assessments can be effective, depending on the purpose. Testing vocabulary terms? Ensuring comprehension? Holding students accountable for doing the pre-class reading? In these and similar scenarios, an LMS or publisher quizzes can be quite appropriate. But to measure students' ability to critically think, analyze, synthesize, and create? Probably not.

Just the other day I had a conversation with a friend and colleague about her son's online high school English class. As someone with a PhD in literature, she was horrified that all the assessments in the class were multiple-choice. How can students learn to think and write, she argued, if they never have to write? And, by implication, if they never have to think?

She has a point. Harried instructors of ever-larger classes have resorted to using auto-graded assessments because they are quick and easy. But I don't think it's the only choice.

Specifications grading to the rescue

We are not locked into using auto-graded quizzes that target the lowest levels of Bloom's taxonomy. Using specifications grading, we can design meaningful and authentic assessments that put the work of learning squarely where it should be: on the students.

Linda Nilson describes this approach in *Specifications Grading: Restoring Rigor, Motivating Students, and Saving Faculty Time* (2014). That sounded too good to be true, so I read the book and subsequently decided to apply this approach in my online graduate-level technology fluency class.

You see, I had a problem. I was and am convinced that students won't do the reading if there are no points attached. So I give them a quiz to make sure they do the reading.

But a multiple-choice quiz, one that targets the lower levels of Bloom's taxonomy, is truly not appropriate for a graduate-level course. Students at this level should demonstrate advanced thinking skills. They should read critically. Analyze. Apply the concepts to their own experiences. A typical multiple-choice quiz doesn't help them to do any of those things.

My online graduate students are working professionals, juggling the demands of school, family, and work. If there's no accountability, they won't do the readings. Sorry, but it's true.

When I came across this grading solution, I decided to try it. Spoiler alert: it worked. Really well.

How specs grading solved my problem

Like many of our teaching and learning methods, there are many ways to apply Nilson's grading strategy. I'll share with you what I did in the hopes of giving you ideas for your own classes.

I used specs grading to design assignments that cause students to think deeply, evaluate, synthesize, and write critically—without overburdening me with the grading. A basic tenet of specs grading is that such tasks are graded on an all-or-nothing approach. If students do the work, if they meet all the assignment criteria, or specifications, they earn 100 percent. If they don't, it's a zero.

Sounds harsh, right? I'll agree that it's a bit risky. It forces us as instructors to provide really detailed instructions, to list exactly what the assignment must include. Nilson compares it to software engineering. A customer provides specifications for the product they require. If some of the specs are met but not all, the production does not move forward. Instead, it goes back to the drawing board until all the specs are met.

So it is with specs grading. If the submission does not meet all specifications, it earns a zero.

Nilson is quick to encourage the use of "oops tokens," one or more opportunities that allow students to learn from their mistake and try again, to resubmit the assignment knowing that this time they must ensure all specs are met. In this way, specs grading develops a growth mindset. Let me tell you, once a student earns a zero instead of the low A or high B they expect, they begin taking the assignment seriously.

In my class, students were assigned to read five of a possible 15 articles for each module. They could choose the ones that were most relevant and interesting to them. For each, they had to write a 200-word response describing what they learned and how it will affect them at work or at home. This produced three to four pages of writing per student per module, enough to be potentially off-putting in terms of grading.

But the written response enabled students to really think about the concepts and apply them to their own experience and context. Exactly what I wanted them to do.

I provided clear instructions and a two-column LMS rubric: *meets expectations* or *does not meet expectations*. Grading their submissions took mere seconds. All I had to do was to quickly read their writing and click-click-click my way through the rubric. They did the work of learning. Not me.

As you can imagine, there was some pushback. But students soon saw that with a fair level of effort, they earned full points on these tasks as opposed to an 87 percent or a 93 percent or some other number picked out of the blue (from a student perspective anyway).

This approach worked for me. I'd encourage you to choose one assessment in your class and give it a whirl. Let's bring back the rigor without killing ourselves with grading.

Reference

Nilson, L. (2015). *Specifications grading: Restoring rigor, motivating students, and saving faculty time*. Stylus Publishing.

Five Types of Quizzes That Deepen Engagement with Course Content

Maryellen Weimer

I've been rethinking my views on quizzing. I'm still not in favor of quizzes that rely on low-level questions where the right answer is a memorized detail or quizzing strategies where the primary motivation is punitive, such as to force students to keep up with the reading. That kind of quizzing doesn't motivate reading for the right reasons, and it doesn't promote deep, lasting learning. But I keep discovering innovative ways faculty are using quizzes, and these practices rest on different premises. I thought I'd use this post to briefly share some of them.

Mix up the structure. Elizabeth Tropman makes a strong case for reading quizzes. She changes up quiz structures on a regular basis. Sometimes it's the usual objective questions, other times it's short-answer questions, or it might be a question that asks for an opinion response to the reading. Some quizzes are open book; a few are take-home. What an interesting way to give students experience responding to different kinds of test questions and to keep quiz experiences from becoming stale.

Reference: Tropman, E., (2014). In defense of reading quizzes. *International Journal of Teaching and Learning in Higher Education, 26*(1), 140–146. https://files.eric.ed.gov/fulltext/EJ1043037.pdf

Collaborative quizzing. Lots of different options are being used here. Students do the quiz, turn it over, stand up and talk with a partner, to others in a small group, or with whomever they choose. After the discussion, they return to their quiz and may change any of their answers. Alternatively, students do the quiz individually, turn it in, and then do the same quiz in a small group. The two quiz scores are combined with the individual score counting for 75 percent of the grade and the group quiz 25 percent (or some other weighted variation). Collaborative quizzing is an effective way to generate enthusiastic discussion of course content and reduce test anxiety.

Reference: Pandey, C., & Kapitanoff, S. (2011). The influence of anxiety and quality of interaction on collaborative test performance. *Active Learning in Higher Education, 12*(3), 163–174. https://doi.org/10.1177/1469787411415077

Quizzing with resources. Students take detailed notes on the reading because they're allowed to use those notes during the quiz. The same approach works with quizzes that cover content presented during class. Students may use their class notes while taking the quizzes. The payoff is a good (or better) set of notes for use during exam preparation. Ali Resaei reports that open-note quizzing coupled with collaboration resulted in significantly higher final exam scores in his quantitative research methods course.

Reference: Rezaei, A. R., (2015). Frequent collaborative quiz taking and conceptual learning. *Active Learning in Higher Education, 16*(3), 187–196. https://doi.org/10.1177/1469787415589627

Quizzing after questioning. Before the quiz occurs, students are given the opportunity to ask questions about potential quiz content. The instructor and the class work on finding the right answer or discussing the merits of possible responses. If someone asks a question that stimulates a lot of good discussion, that question becomes the quiz question, and students have the designated amount of time to write an answer. Or if a variety of good questions have been asked, answered, and discussed by a variety of students, the professor who shared this option may tell students they've just had their quiz and everyone present gets full credit. This approach encourages students to ask better questions and facilitates substantive classroom discussions.

Online quizzes completed before class. Students complete an online quiz before class. The quizzes are graded electronically with a compiled summary going to the professor so there's enough time to look at the most frequently missed problems or identify areas of misunderstanding (or both). Then class time can be used to address those concepts that are giving students the most trouble.

The advantage of regular quizzes is that they provide ongoing opportunities for retrieval practice and much cognitive psychology research (like that summarized in the reference that follows) documents the benefits of frequent testing. Regular quizzing does improve class attendance, and it gets more students coming to class prepared. Those are not trivial benefits, but with a few different design features, quizzes can also promote deeper engagement with the content, further the development of important learning skills, and provide teachers and students with feedback that promotes learning.

Reference: Brame, C. J., & Biel, R., (2015). Test-enhanced learning: The potential for testing to promote greater learning in undergraduate science courses. *Cell Biology Education—Life Sciences Education, 14*(2), es4. https://doi.org/10.1187/cbe.14-11-0208

Doing More with Formative Assessments

Maryellen Weimer

Authors Kulasegaram and Rangachari (2018) propose moving beyond our understanding of formative assessments as "interim measures" that lead to the real, final assessments—the ones that generate the all-important grades. They suggest we stop calling them formative assessments and start thinking about them as assessments for learning. "We contend that assessment for meaningful learning should prepare students not just to get good grades and meet the requirements of a specific course, but give them the training, the skills, and the enthusiasm for the long haul" (p. 5).

They support this new vision of formative assessment by pointing out how inadequately most summative assessments measure competence. Their context is medical education, but the points they make relate to the preparation of all kinds of professionals. Testing factual recall is easy, and its methods are objective, but there are pedagogical costs. "Important learning outcomes, such as the ability of students to extrapolate their knowledge or apply it to novel problems . . . are lost. Moreover, poor learning behaviors are reinforced in students, including the tendency to gorge on knowledge immediately before assessment and followed by a quick purge as the students move on to the next assessment" (p. 6).

Assessments for learning should accomplish a "judicious mix" (p. 9) of the following. They should (1) help learners see where they are in meeting course objectives; (2) identify what they haven't learned or still need to learn; (3) enable them to transfer their knowledge and skills to novel situations; (4) promote a deeper understanding of the material; and (5) provide them an opportunity to personalize their learning. These assessments can take place at several different levels in an educational experience. They can happen in the classroom; at the level of the course (meaning they build individual class sessions and course topics into a coherent, integrated whole); and at the programmatic level.

Interesting points are made about the need for rigor in assessment for learning. Formative assessments are often referred to as "low-stakes," and that's fine, but that shouldn't be conflated with "low quality." If an assessment is to promote learning it must reinforce what's being learned, provide feedback on both the content and the learning, and direct the learner to resources that can be helpful with improvement.

Feedback that promotes learning is "actionable." It offers the learner things they can do that respond to what they have done. Receiving feedback, particularly if it's critical, can cause learners to self-protect. This means those delivering the feedback must be concerned about the content, how the feedback is delivered, and what's identified as in need of improvement.

Although this discussion of assessment for learning is abstract, it does include a number of concrete examples, among them some not often considered, like oral exams. If students are permitted to select the topics, oral exams offer a powerful way for individualizing learning. Student knowledge can be probed in ways not possible on paper exams. And the oral exam makes cheating and plagiarism moot. The primary objective of learning assessments is not grade generation. The feedback enables the student to monitor where they are on the way to meeting the course objectives. So, if the oral exam is something more like an oral review session, it might not be as anxiety-provoking.

Moreover, the authors are aware that factors like class size, faculty-student ratios in a program, the layout of classrooms, and the available time all have implications in terms of what can be accomplished. Assessment for learning at its best is a time-consuming endeavor. However, the benefits of assessment for learning are worth accomplishing even in bits. If oral exams are not feasible, a collection or even a few individualized exam questions, possibly selected from a question set proposed by the student, can provide the student a novel learning experience. "Meaningful learning can be significantly enhanced if students were given an opportunity to personalize their learning" (p. 6).

It's an interesting article that does propose a different and definitely more substantive way of thinking about formative assessment. Not only does it require a change of attitude and understanding on the part of the teacher, it would require considerable reordering in how students think about assessment. Considering it makes sense when we remember that assessment drives learning: how learning is assessed determines what students will learn and how they will learn it.

Reference

Kulasegaram, K., & Rangachari, P. (2018). Beyond "formative": Assessment to enrich student learning. *Advances in Physiology Education, 42*(1), 5–14. https://doi.org/10.1152/advan.00122.2017

Writing Better Multiple-Choice Questions

Jim Sibley

Eleven years ago, I discovered a life-changing pedagogy called team-based learning. It let me do things in large classrooms that I didn't think was possible. I found that the key to successful team-based learning was writing really good multiple-choice questions. I would like to look at the multiple-choice format overall, including some of the vocabulary we use when looking at the literature on writing multiple-choice questions.

Over the years my beliefs around multiple-choice questions have evolved. Bob Bjork's article "Multiple-Choice Questions Exonerated at Least of Some Charges" points to multiple-choice questions as really good vehicles to enhance learning. We often think that short-answer questions are the answer because in a multiple-choice question, the student needs only to recognize the right answer rather than retrieve it. Bjork's studies have revealed that multiple-choice questions strengthen the student's understanding of all the presented options, not just the single correct retrieval. His main idea is that multiple-choice questions have a really valuable place in learning. While they might not have a valuable place in assessment all of the time, in learning, multiple choice questions are really quite excellent.

Anatomy of a multiple-choice question

The question at the top, the actual question part of a multiple-choice question is called the *stem* or sometimes the *question leader*. The various answers, A, B, C, D, are known as the *options*. The options contain the correct answer and the incorrect answers. The correct answers are often referred to as *keyed responses* in the literature. The incorrect answers are referred to as *distractors* or *foils*.

Developing stems

The first step in writing good questions is deciding what is test-worthy knowledge. This is a place where instructors often fail when writing multiple-choice questions. We will start writing questions without thinking about what the students truly need to know. If you jump straight to writing questions, you tend to write questions at a very low level. If you step back a bit and identify the most important test-worthy knowledge, you can start writing questions at a higher level.

In developing stems, it's helpful to write a standalone question. There are many examples of excellent multiple-choice questions that aren't standalone, but that's the gold standard, to try to make it a standalone question. A student should be able to put their hands over the options and successfully answer the question if it's well-written. The stem should be grammatically complete and as clear as possible for the student.

Also, avoid negative stems if possible. If using negative words in the stem, you'll want to bold them or underline them. The question should not be tricky. You want to make sure you're testing the student's understanding of the contents, not their ability to read the questions, so make bold or underline any "not" or negative statements.

Developing the options

There are a number of rules regarding option development. First, keep the options as short as possible. What you may often find is that, as you write the options, a phrase will consistently appear in the options. You don't want long, rambling options because you can make the question tricky just by the length of the option.

Make sure there is a correct answer that's clearly and defensibly the best, as well as incorrect answers that are clearly incorrect. There is a line you may be straddling there, as we want to make options plausible enough that we are testing the student's understanding.

If options start to cluster around the correct end of the spectrum, you've created a question that will likely make the student mad. Try to avoid using "all" or "none of the above," mostly because the question should test higher-level understanding, and nothing is absolute once you get to higher levels.

We also want to keep the options similar in length so we don't kind of give away any hints on what might be the right answer. Just like when writing lists, use parallel construction. Ensure grammatical consistency and make sure that there are not any cues in that question stem that are going to help students eliminate some of the options.

Construction errors

There are some very common errors that we all make as we write questions. The most common errors are grammatical cues. For example, you write a singular stem with a singular answer and a plural option. A test-wise student, if they don't know the answer, will use that grammatical cue to guess more effectively.

Another one we often see is that in writing a series of options, the correct answer and some incorrect answers, and you'll write a little more detail around the correct option so it really truly is correct. Again, a test-wise student will pick up on this. And if one of the options is longer than the others, they'll guess that one, hoping that you have fallen into this trap.

Another place we can get ourselves into trouble is having logic cues called overlapping options. Repeating words is another one we often do. We'll take a phrase or a word from the stem, and we'll reuse it in one of the options.

There's another human tendency as we develop multiple-choice questions to put the correct answer as option B or C. This is especially true when we write numerical questions with a numerical list. For some reason, we often don't like to make the answer the first one or the last one because that's "too obvious." So be aware of this as you write your questions.

Take the time to write good questions

So have a talk with yourself, and make sure you spend the time to write good questions. The good news? You can write good questions with effort. The bad news: the better you get at writing multiple-choice questions, the longer it will take to write good questions. But in the end, writing good questions is well worth the time and effort involved.

Group Exams and Quizzes: Design Options to Consider

Maryellen Weimer

Although still not at all that widely used, there's long-standing interest in letting students work together on quizzes or exams. Upon first hearing about the approach, teachers' initial response is almost always negative. Here are the most common **objections**.

- **Grades are measures of individual mastery of material.** With a group exam or quiz, some students may get a better grade than they've earned. Group grades do not measure individual learning.
- **A group can settle on wrong answers** and thereby lower the score of the single bright student in the group who knows the right answer.
- **Group exams and quizzes make it too easy** for students. They don't have to think for themselves but can rely on others in the group to do the thinking for them.
- **It's cheating.** Students are getting answers they don't know from other students. They're consulting another source rather than putting in the work and developing their own knowledge.
- **Certifying exams** (various professional exams such as those in nursing, accounting, the MCAT and GRE, for example) **are not group exams.** Group quizzes and exams do not prepare students for these all-important assessments.

At the same time, those who do allow group collaboration on exams and quizzes may respond to the objections with a corresponding set of set of **advantages** associated with their use.

- **Group exams and quizzes reduce test anxiety.** Pretty much across the board, students report that anticipating and participating in group exams and quizzes makes them feel less anxious. And for students with exam anxiety, that can be a significant benefit.

- **Collaborative quizzes and exams show students that they can learn from each other.** Many students arrive in courses believing the only person they can learn from is the teacher. But as they talk about test questions, share answer justifications, and discuss what content the answer requires, they get to experience what it's like to learn from peers.
- **Group quizzes and exams provide immediate feedback.** Students don't have to wait to get the exam back. They get a good indication from those in the group why the answer is or is not correct.
- **Working together on test questions teaches students how to identify credible arguments and sources.** Given the opportunity to change answers based on what someone else says directly confronts students with the tough issues of who to believe and when to trust their own judgment.
- **Collaborative quizzes and exams model how problem solving in professional contexts usually occurs.** Professionals collaborate, have access to resources, can contact experts, argue options, and evaluate possible answers. Collaborative testing gives students the opportunity to see how and why that results in better decision making.
- **Group quizzes and exams can improve exam scores and sometimes, but not always, content retention.** The improvement in scores is an expected outcome of collaboration, but the improvement is also present when students collaborate on exam questions and then answer questions that deal with the same content on a subsequent exam taken individually. Effects of collaboration on retention are mixed. See the following references listed at the end of this article for examples: Cortright et al. (2002), Gilley and Clarkson (2014), Leight et al. (2012), Lust and Conklin (2003), and Woody et al. (2008).

Group/collaborative exam design options

The faculty who use group exam and quiz options also answer the concerns with a variety of different design options. Many of these options address the common objections mentioned earlier or work around them in ways that protect the integrity of assessment experiences.

- Use small groups, three or four students, even partners. The smaller the group, the greater the pressure to share and the harder it is to let everyone else in the group come up with the answers. Peer pressure is a powerful motivator. Most students do not want to look unprepared or stupid in front of their peers. In the Pandy and Kapitanoff (2011) design, on given exam days only 50 percent of the students collaborate. They work in pairs, but before they arrive in class they do not know whether they will be taking the exam individually or working on it with a partner. Randomly assigning partners motivates preparation (Lusk & Conklin, 2003).

- Don't give group grades; use individual grades but allow the students a designated time for collaboration. Students first take the exam, then they meet with their group to discuss questions they couldn't answer or weren't sure about. They're then given a brief amount of time to change how they answered those questions, if they believe the answer can be improved. See Hoke and Robbins (2005) for an example of how this works.

If students change their original answer but mark their new answer with a different color ink, during the debrief, the issue of who you believe and when you trust yourself can be raised in the context whether the changed answers were correct or wrong.

If it's an essay exam, the collaboration may occur before students start writing. See Shindler (2004) for an example.

- Control the content of the collaboration. Say it's a 50-question multiple-choice test. Students do 40 questions individually. They jointly answer the remaining 10 questions. See Kapitanoff (2009) for discussion of how this approach works.
- Reverse the order of the collaboration using it as an exam preparation activity. Students work collaboratively on an open-book-and-notes take-home essay exam. Immediately after turning in the group exam, they take an objective, in-class exam individually. Both exams may count, but perhaps not equally. Sroug et al. (2013) explain how this worked in a molecular biotechnology course.
- Give a grade that combines the individual and group grades. Students take the exam, turn it in and then do the same exam as a group. Their individual grade counts for 80 percent of their grade with 20 percent coming from the group grade. You also could use a 60–40 or 50–50 ratio. Some faculty discourage group participation without preparation by stipulating that a failing individual exam score prevents addition of the group score. See Clinton and Kohlmeyer (2005) and Slusser and Erickson (2006) for these grading options.

- If you're interested in collaboration on test questions but unsure of the logistics or maybe doubtful of the benefits, start out by letting students work together on a low-stakes quiz.

Group/collaborative exam and quiz resources

Here's a collection of references that showcase these design variations and the range of disciplines where collaborative testing has been used.

Clinton, D. B., & Kohlmeyer, J. M., III. (2005). The effects of group quizzes on performance and motivation to learn. *Journal of Accounting Education, 23*(2), 96–116.

- Students did the quizzes individually first and then completed a group quiz. The student's quiz grade was the average of their individual score and the group score.

Cortright, R. N., Collins, H. L., Rodenbaugh, D. W., & DiCarlo, S. E. (2003). Student retention of course content is improved by collaborative-group testing. *Advances in Physiology Education, 27*(3), 102–108.

- Students partner to answer selected exam questions then answered that question set as part of subsequent exam. "Results suggest that collaborative testing is an effective strategy to enhance learning and increase student retention of course content" (p. 102).

Gilley, B. H., & Clarkston, B. (2014). Collaborative testing: Evidence of learning in a controlled in-class study of undergraduate students. *Journal of College Science Teaching, 43*(3), 83–91.

- Students who took individual tests after group tests had higher scores than students who took individual tests twice.

Giuliodori, M. J., Lujan, H. L., & DiCarolo, S. E. (2009). Student interaction characteristics during collaborative group testing. *Advances in Physiology Education, 33*(Summer), 24–29.

- Analysis revealed that high performing students did not answer for the rest of the group.

Hoke, M. M., & Robbins, L. K., (2005). The impact of active learning on nursing students' clinical success. *Journal of Holistic Nursing, 32*(4), 348–355.

- An example of how students do the exam on their own but then have the opportunity to collaborate with others about answers. After they've talked with others, students can change their individual answers.

Knierim, K., Turner, H., & Davis, R. K. (2015). Two-stage exams improve student learning in an introductory geology course: Logistics, attendances and grades. *Journal of Geoscience Education, 63*(2), 157–164.

- The use of a collaborative exam option improved attendance by 16 percent compared with sections without collaboration.

Kapitanoff, S. H. (200). Collaborative testing: Cognitive and interpersonal processes related to enhanced test performance. *Active Learning in Higher Education, 10*(1), 56–70.

- Controlled the questions over which students collaborated on the exam.

Leight, H., Saunders, C., Calkins, R., & Withers, M. (2012). Collaborative testing improves performance but not content retention in a large-enrollment introductory biology class. *Cell Biology Education—Life Science Education, 11*(4), 392–303.

- Exams after group collaboration had cumulative test questions, and students who had a group experience did not score better than those who had not taken a group exam.

LoGiudice, A. B., Pachai, A. A., & Kim, J. A. (2015). Testing together: When do student learn more through collaborative tests? *Scholarship of Teaching and Learning in Psychology, 1*(4), 377–389.

- Reviewed the research in search of answers to two questions: what memory mechanisms are at play when students test in groups, and when collaborative testing is most likely to enhance learning above and beyond individual testing.

Lusk, M., & Conklin, L. (2003). Collaborative testing to promote learning. *Journal of Nursing Education, 42*(3), 121–124.

- Students work alone and then collaborate with a randomly assigned partner. They may change their answers based on the collaboration. Found collaboration did not benefit long-term retention.

Pandey, C., & Kapitanoff, S. (2011). The influence of anxiety and quality of interaction on collaborative test performance. *Active Learning in Higher Education, 12*(3), 163–174.

- Used an interesting technique to motivate exam preparation. Fifty percent took the exam individually; 50 percent took it with a partner. Students didn't know whether they'd have a partner until they arrived for the test. Those who collaborated were chosen randomly as were their partners.

Rao, S. P., Collins, H. L, & DiCarlo, S. E. (2002). Collaborative testing enhances student learning. *Advances in Physiology Education, 26*(1), 37–41.

- Students in a physiology course took four different types of quizzes individually and then in groups.

Russo, A., & Warren, S. H. (1999). Collaborative test taking. *College Teaching, 47*(1), 18–20.

- A student and teacher recount their first experiences with collaborative testing in an English course.

Shindler, J. V. (2004). "Greater than the sum of the parts?" Examining the soundness of collaborative exams in teacher education courses. *Innovative Higher Education, 28*(4), 273–283.

- Found collaborative exams were valid, reliable, and efficient and had positive effects on learners.

Slusser, S. R., & Erickson, R. J. (2006). Group quizzes: An extension of the collaborative learning process. *Teaching Sociology, 34*(3), 249–262.

- Students completed quizzes with two to three open-ended questions. Then they talked about their answers in a group, adjusting their answers as they saw fit. One quiz was randomly selected from the group, and the grade on that quiz was received by everyone in the group.

Sroug, M. C., Miller, H. B., Witherow, D. S., & Carson, S. (2013). Assessment of a novel group-centered testing scheme in an upper-level undergraduate molecular biotechnology course. *Biochemistry and Molecular Biology Education, 41*(4), 232–241.

- Students collaborated on an open-book, take-home essay exam before taking an objective exam individually.

Weimer, M. (2013). *Learner-centered teaching: Five key changes to practice* (2nd ed.). Jossey-Bass. (See pages 81–83.)

- Recounts experiences with group exams, particularly their success at getting students engaged in deep conversations about course content.

Woody, W. D., Woody, L. K., & Bromley, S. (2008). Anticipated group versus individual examinations: A classroom comparison. *Teaching of Psychology, 35*(1), 13–17.

- Collaboration via active discussion before individual testing improved test scores but not retention.

From Traditional to Cyber CATS: Different Breeds for Different Needs

Amanda Hurlbut and Karen Dunlap

Research has shown that using formative assessment to inform instruction is one of the most important components of good teaching (Rosenshine, 2012). While many teachers rely solely on questioning and discussion techniques to gauge a class's comprehension and learning, formative assessment strategies are needed to engage and assess learners individually. Classroom assessment techniques (CATs) facilitate more meaningful learning by providing opportunities for students to self-reflect on their learning while instructors collect information on what and to what degree students learned (Angelo & Cross, 1993). Here are three fresh takes on CATs and how they can be used in online courses.

Breed one: discussion CATs

Classroom instructors have long known that one of the best ways to assess students' understanding of content is to get them talking. But typical Q&A formats can be routine and boring. *On the line* is a technique that overcomes this problem. First, the teacher constructs a series of opposing statements about a topic related to class learning. These statements should be designed to spark debate and deep thinking, and students must formulate their agreement with or other opinion on the matter using information from the class period or about the topic discussed. The teacher then asks students to place themselves, according to their preference, on an imaginary line that spans the length of a classroom. In the teaching field, for example, the instructor could ask, "Which is more important to driving student learning: engaging activities or formative assessment?" The answer, of course, is both, but allowing students to choose one side helps to facilitate deep thinking and rationalization. Alternately, students who do not have a strong opinion on the matter can put themselves in the neutral, middle zone of the line. When we introduce this activity, we start out with sample statements, such as "Which type of snack do you prefer: sweet or salty?" We then gradually work up to more difficult topics that involve basic understandings of what we've discussed in class.

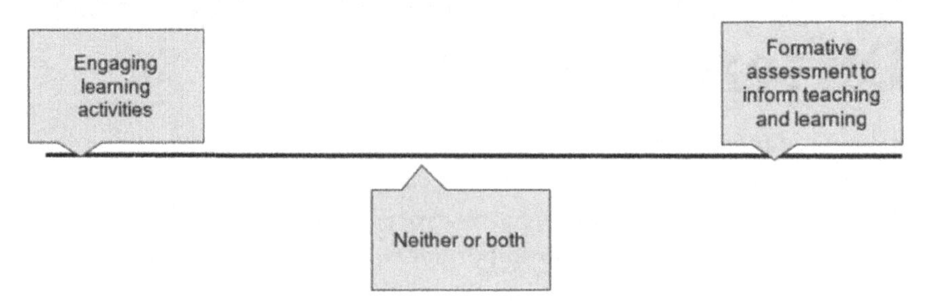

While this is a great strategy to use during face-to-face (F2F) classes, how can it be done online? One answer is Flipgrid. Flipgrid hosts social media–inspired video discussion boards. In online classes, students are traditionally required to post written questions or responses (or both) to questions on a digital discussion board. Flipgrid utilizes the ease of taking videos with smartphones and other devices. Students access the grid board, view the prompt, and then record a brief oral response that is posted. This allows the students to both state where they stand and why. The video can be rerecorded and saved as many times as the student wishes before being posted. Students can then view others' videos and record responses to them. The video format encourages engagement with the topic.

Breed two: interactive CATs

Interactive CATs are forms of assessment that allow students to actively engage with the content during rather than after a learning session. This can take many forms, such as students' holding up index cards to demonstrate either-or relationships; drawing or illustrating concept maps to show patterns and relationships; writing responses to questions or generating examples and nonexamples on whiteboards and holding them up for the instructor to see; and completing interactive, multiple-choice quizzes using a game format. The main point of these types of CATs is to facilitate active learning through a lesson while also letting the instructor check for the entire class's understanding before proceeding with a lesson.

Nearpod is a tool that can encompass many features of interactive CATs in one and can be used in both F2F and online settings. Nearpod is a web application that allows instructors to create teaching presentations interspersed with quizzes, open-ended responses, drawing boards, drag-and-drop items, polls, and collaborative posts that students submit throughout the presentation. Not only do these activities offer students opportunities to engage with the content and in learning, they also provide instructors with formative assessment data that can be used to give feedback. In a F2F setting, instructors can use student response apps to collect real-time examples of concepts; display exemplars of student work to the class; and quickly clarify, correct, and enhance understanding of the content where student responses indicate a lack of understanding. In an online setting, students can use Nearpod in the student-paced mode, in which they asynchronously access the material, including the interactions, on their own time and even receive instant feedback on answers, such as what the correct response is and why.

Breed three: reflective CATs

Exit tickets are a great way to facilitate reflection about content at the end of a class period. One of our favorite exit ticket ideas is a connected, reflective process known as *teaching synectics*. In this model, students learn to use a new idea or course concept and connect it metaphorically with the visual image of a well-known idea or topic. For instance, in a pedagogy class for preservice teachers, students are taught about differentiation and meeting individual student learning needs. They are given a variety of images and directed to reflect on what they've learned about the educational process connected to the image by verbalizing or writing their observations on the back of the image, as in the example below:

No two people have the same exact physical or emotional needs. This idea is no different for students in a classroom. Because every child is unique, they will also have their own set of needs in relation to learning, behavior and discipline, and even their emotions. No two paint brushes are the same. Some brushes have stains from past projects they worked on. Others may still have old paint on their bristles. New paint brushes have straight bristles with no spots on them. Many students come into a classroom well rested, fed, and ready to work. Unfortunately, not every student has this story. Some students have a harder home life and come into the classroom with scars from their past. Other students behave poorly because they've never been taught otherwise. A teacher must enter their classroom knowing that some students may need more instruction, others more structure, and some will simply need more encouragement. Similarly, no two paint brushes create the same stroke. An artist will learn this and use each brush how it will be most effective in their painting. When looking at brushes one on one, it can be seen that each has its own purpose. Though some are of similar size, or of similar materials, or even similar shape, each is used to create a specific line. People may share qualities, personality traits, or physical characteristics, but each will have aspects of their person that makes them different. Teachers must pay attention to their students' needs and figure out how to make the classroom an environment that will foster learning in each student, much like how an artist must use their brushes how they are best suited to complete a painting. One teaching style will not effectively convey every concept to every student. Because of this, teachers must be aware of how their students learn and their individual needs. An artist requires many different paint brushes to make a single painting. Without the variety, the painting would not be as detailed or sophisticated. Without each student, the class would lose potential to be a positive learning environment. The differences in each student allows others to hear new ideas, meet a wider variety of people, and gain social skills.

—Student example, used with permission

Seesaw is an app that allows students to create and submit a variety of types of content, such as videos, images, drawings, documents, and portfolios of objects. It is our favorite way to convert exit tickets, teaching synectics, and other reflections to online environments through the journal feature. Students are given a reflection prompt related to course content and reply to this prompt in Seesaw. They can write a reflection, include a link to a website or article, post or annotate a picture, or record an audio or video reflection.

This tool lends itself to easily converting the teaching synectics exit ticket because it allows for creativity and variety in the reflection formats. To us, the absolute best feature of Seesaw is that when a student posts a reflection in the class journal, the instructor can provide immediate feedback by typing or recording an audio comment. This facilitates classroom assessment as a formative tool to further true learning.

CATs are important hallmarks of the teaching and learning process. By incorporating innovative and creative ways of assessing students' understanding and engaging them with the content, instructors can better facilitate deep reflection on new learning. Assessment is just as important in online environments as in traditional ones, and emerging technology can assist instructors in designing these engaging experiences for students.

References

Angelo, T., & Cross, P. K. (1993). *Classroom assessment techniques: A handbook for college teachers* (2nd ed.). Jossey-Bass.

Rosenshine, B. (2012). Principles of instruction: Research based strategies that all teachers should know. *American Educator, 36*(1), 12.

Formative Assessment Techniques for Online Learning

Emily Faulconer and Beverly Wood

While most faculty think of assessments as used to measure learning after the fact, formative assessment classroom techniques (FACTs) give an instructor a snapshot of where students are in their learning so as to address any gaps in their understanding. Online instructors have a variety of tools at their disposal to incorporate engaging FACTs into their courses to improve learning outcomes.

Partner questioning rounds are a discussion forum strategy that both measures student learning and forces students to approach the course content with a questioning mind. Students are put into pairs, with each given its own discussion forum. Students then take turns asking each other questions they have about the course material, with the other student answering. Students do three rounds of questions, and so this technique can be spread out across a weeklong online module, with one student assigned to ask a question on Monday, Wednesday, and Friday and the other assigned to ask a question on Tuesday, Thursday, and Saturday. In this way students are asking and answering questions as their understanding develops throughout the module. The process thus allows instructors to see how student understanding is or is not developing and how students are interpreting the course content.

Think-pair-share (TPS) is another discussion forum strategy that tasks students to work together to solve a problem or answer a question. This strategy also requires dividing students into pairs. First, students think individually about the topic or question and then share their ideas with their partner. Pairing students helps because many are more likely to engage when they are working in a semiprivate area, outside of the larger online discussion forum visible to all students. The structure of this FACT also encourages individual accountability for engagement.

This strategy could be applied in an English course where students contemplate a prompt about a specific excerpt or piece then exchange ideas with a partner to prepare a response to the whole group. The instructor can monitor the pairs for productive exchange of ideas and be prepared for the disparities or consistencies when the pairs share with the whole class. The FACT could also be used in a mathematics course to allow students to share their strategies for solving problems. Instructors could then observe the different processes students used and gather information on the most common strategies used successfully as well as common errors and misconceptions.

Annotated student drawings is a FACT that allows students to apply their understanding to images. Student first either create or find an image related to the course content. They then annotate that image to represent concepts covered in the course. For example, in an engineering course exploring wastewater treatment, students could be required to either find or create an image of a wastewater treatment system. Some students will prefer to use their graphic design skills to create a drawing, while others will find one on the internet. Then students would be required to sketch out the various steps in wastewater treatment by adding labels to the image that represent those steps. They can do this by using free photo-editing software such as Pixorize, Pixlr, or PicMonkey or meme generating websites such as Meme Generator (https://imgflip.com/memegenerator) or Meme Creator (http://www.memecreator.org/create). Most students today are well versed in annotating images and creating memes.

Using this strategy early in a lesson gives the instructor insight into prior knowledge, while using it later in a lesson provides an opportunity to evaluate misconceptions and vocabulary use. If used early in the module, the annotated image could be revisited later in the module with a reflective prompt and the opportunity to edit based on feedback.

3-2-1 is an excellent FACT to use as an exit ticket in either traditional or asynchronous classrooms. While this FACT has several variations, the common theme is that students prepare three key ideas, two vocabulary words with definitions, and one question they still have. These can be submitted as ordinary text documents using the assignment feature of an LMS or gathered with a tool such as Google Forms. A form can be set up with fields to fill out, with the results automatically compiled and presented to the instructor to determine where the class stands on the material. The instructor can use the information to craft a wrap-up announcement for the module that answers the student questions or to develop extra content or work to address common issues.

While clickers have garnered significant attention in traditional classrooms, particularly those with large enrollments, **online polls** can serve the same function in an asynchronous online course. PollEverywhere even has the capability to embed the poll directly into the LMS and report the live results. Polling is truly versatile and can be used to check for basic content understanding, explore prior knowledge or common misconceptions, or to gauge opinions. For example, in a biomechanics course, the poll could quickly determine whether students can identify a specific muscle by name. This poll can also be open throughout the module to measure student learning at different points as they go through the content. The fact that the poll is not graded and feeds only one or two questions at a time makes it less anxiety-inducing than graded assessments. Students can use their results to determine where they misunderstood something and need to go back to look at the material again.

A **terminology inventory probe** (TIP) can be used as an introduction activity in an online module to gauge student prior knowledge and misconceptions. In this FACT, students are presented with key vocabulary and asked to identify whether they (1) have never heard of the word, (2) have heard of the word but are unsure of the definition, (3) have an idea of what the word means, or (4) know what it means and can define it. This FACT could be programmed into the LMS as a quiz or an unweighted survey. Alternatively, it could be embedded into the LMS using H5P, a free, open-source platform that allows the completion of the TIP to be graded as pass-fail for participation.

Sorting activities are an engaging alternative to the traditional quizzing format. In a meteorology course, for example, students may be tasked with sorting gases by whether they are greenhouse gases. Online card sorting tools are freemium-based, with the free version allowing only a limited amount of time on the system or permitting only a restricted number of participants. Paying the premium cost removes these restrictions. However, there are some off-line card sorting tools that are free to use but require software downloads, including UXSORT, Uzilla Mozdev, and WebCat.

Formative assessment is an underutilized method of determining where online students stand in understanding material. Luckily, there are a variety of tools and techniques available to the online instructor to measure student understanding and intervene where needed to improve learning outcomes.

Part 5

Making Your Course Accessible

UDL: A Powerful Framework

Gwen Bass and Michael Lawrence-Riddell

Increasingly, instructors at the college level are called upon to create classroom learning experiences that can be characterized using terms like *academically rigorous, accessible, differentiated, trauma-sensitive, inclusive, culturally relevant,* and *student-centered.* While teaching faculty are generally regarded as content experts, supporting the diverse array of learning needs represented in our courses can prove challenging. Moreover, there is a growing expectation that we also teach 21st-century skills and prepare students for values-driven professional work, all the while maintaining accountability, encouraging effort over outcome, and implementing equitable and transparent grading practices. Institutions are finding creative ways to equip faculty with resources to meet these demands, and yet this remains an incredibly tall order in the context of higher education as we know it.

Enter universal design for learning (UDL). This powerful framework for educators centers on three principles that align with neuroscientific research on the networks that affect learning. Through UDL, educators reach all students by using the following:

1. **Multiple means of representation.** Give learners various ways of acquiring information and knowledge.
2. **Multiple means of expression.** Provide learners alternatives for demonstrating what they know.
3. **Multiple means of engagement.** Tap into learners' interests, offer appropriate challenges, and increase motivation (Kurzweil Education, n.d.).

Implementing UDL requires anticipating a range of learning needs and embedding scaffolding into the curriculum and course materials that support students through challenges to content mastery and the acquisition of skills you want them to gain or refine—be they content-specific or the 21st-century type that are foundational to innovation, creativity, and professional achievement in today's workforce.

UDL is grounded in research demonstrating that students who are engaged perform at higher levels (McClenney et al., 2012), that people learn in different ways, and that everyone's path to the classroom is different. Students within a given classroom will have varying levels of comfort and readiness for assigned tasks. For example, a student who lacks prior content knowledge in one subject may be an expert in another. Similarly, when it comes to the learning process, some students in a classroom may have extensive experience and exposure to the research process, while others may need explicit teaching on how to do an assignment before they can complete it successfully. When students are provided multiple points of entry to course material and assignments, academic engagement and outcomes improve, and educators uphold their responsibility to create a classroom culture that mimics that of the professional workplace, where leaders seek to fuel innovation by hiring employees who know how to collaborate, examine issues from multiple perspectives, and communicate creatively.

UDL is commonly adopted at the pre-K–12 level, especially given shifts in special education funding, but it has been slower to gain traction in the college classroom. Many educators consider UDL an "alternative model" that requires us to redesign our classes to benefit students who "learn differently" rather than an approach that could serve *all* students in their pursuit of knowledge and preparation for the world of work. Research on innovation in the corporate context demonstrates that all markers of success in the business world hinge not only upon inherent diversity (that is, employing individuals with a range of fixed identity traits), but also, and more importantly, on cultural practices that value and promote the inclusion of multiple perspectives. If one of our goals in higher education is to offer training that facilitates a smooth transition into the workforce, we actually owe it to all of our students to create learning environments that are inclusive of inherent diversity and to explicitly teach them how to engage authentically, how to innovate, and how to communicate across lines of difference.

Practically applied, suppose that you typically have students read a book chapter and then quiz them on specific information. Are there podcasts, films, or interactive websites that have similar content? Can you find ways to show your students how this information connects to their lives, their interests, and their prior knowledge? Are there unique applications of this content that students could identify independently or ways that you could ask students to reflect on case studies, practical examples, or personal experiences to integrate the acquired knowledge in context? How can students collaborate in an effort to consider multiple perspectives, communicate their differing ideas about the content through a range of platforms and in various formats, and explore new directions for the application of emerging knowledge? Most importantly, how can our teaching practices demonstrate to our students that by honoring individualized learning paths, we are more positively contributing to the collective than when we apply a one-size-fits-all approach?

Most educators maintain the goal of communicating information to students in order to cultivate passion about the subject matter and inspire them to positively impact the field on a broader scale. When considering the integration of UDL principles in course design, there are two essential questions one must address: What content is critical for students to take away? and What skills am I hoping my students gain or refine through this work? If instructors use these key questions as a lens, or a litmus test, they can plan experiences for their students that allow for multiple means of gaining the information or producing work that conveys their understanding. Herein lies the opportunity for us to think about the application of learning beyond the walls of our classrooms and what we really want students to do with the knowledge and skills they acquire through our courses. When we cultivate a classroom climate that values multiple perspectives by integrating a range of learning exercises and applications, we are not only engaging our students more actively, but we are providing vital preparation for future professional pursuits.

References

Kurzweil Education. (n.d.). Three principles of UDL. https://www.kurzweiledu.com/udl-three-principles-p4.html

McClenney, K., Marti, C. N., & Adkins, C. (2012). *Student engagement and student outcomes: Key findings from CCSSE validation research.* https://www.ccsse.org/aboutsurvey/docs/CCSSE%20Validation%20Summary.pdf

Universal Design in Courses: Beyond Disabilities

Thomas J. Tobin

The concept of universal design for learning (UDL) was initially developed in order to provide equal access to learning opportunities for students in face-to-face courses. It has since been adapted for many learning situations, including online courses. However, there is still a widespread perception that UDL is appropriate only as an accommodation for learners with disabilities. Faculty members are usually not clear about when to adopt universal design strategies, what kind of work UDL entails, and what benefits come out of the process for students and instructors.

A tale of two professors

Professors Carrie Oakey in the music department and Gene Poole in the biology department wanted to enhance their existing online courses beyond the usual lecture notes and a few PowerPoint presentations. They went to the university's teaching and learning center and learned that the law requires accessibility options for nontext multimedia: usually captions or a text-only version.

Professor Oakey and a staffer from the teaching and learning center recorded two videos: one of herself and her graduate students playing a Bach concerto and another of a graduate student singing a Bach cantata. Oakey uploaded the videos into week 3 and week 6 of her online Music 101: The Art of Listening course and created two assignments, asking her students to write a two-page response paper about each performance. Oakey wondered how she would create captions or other access methods for the videos, because the audio content is the whole point of experiencing the videos.

Professor Poole brought one of his 80-slide PowerPoint presentations to the teaching and learning center, where he worked with a staffer to chop up the content into eight 10-slide modules. In order to add an audio component, Professor Poole wrote out a script of what he would say while each slide was displayed to students; then Poole recorded his audio from the script. The teaching and learning center staff created eight movie files that contained Poole's slides, his voice-over, and closed captions (based on Poole's script). Poole uploaded the eight movies into Unit 3 of his online BIO 337: Cell Biology course, along with the scripts themselves to act as text-only alternatives. He then set up a discussion forum to ask his students to write their descriptions of the processes that Poole had outlined in his videos. Poole spent nearly six hours doing the recording, editing, and selecting processes to create one total hour of finished movies, and he wondered whether his investment of so much time would be worth it if he were to update the rest of his materials in a similar way.

Beyond disabilities

Universal design goes beyond just assisting those with disabilities and offers benefits for everyone involved in the online learning environment. By representing information in various ways, an online course designed via UDL provides multiple paths through the course: students can start by watching a short video clip of their professor, print out the text-only version while they are working on an assignment, and then watch the video again with captions turned on while they are studying after the kids have gone to bed.

UDL in online courses also solves what might otherwise be a big problem: noncomputer devices. More online learners today own mobile devices (such as smartphones and tablets) rather than computers (desktops and laptops) (Smith et al., 2011). When profs provide versions of content that are bandwidth-friendly (e.g., text-only scripts or caption sets), learners can consume the content based on their devices' capabilities. Providing multiple versions also frees learners from being dependent on one specific application in order to work with the materials (e.g., requiring students to have PowerPoint versus hosting a short video of the same content on YouTube).

Universal design also fosters creativity and choice for all online learners. By offering students alternative ways of responding to assignments, profs can move beyond the usual "write an essay" method of demonstrating the skills and knowledge that learners acquire. Even providing one alternative for each assignment expands learners' paths through the course. For example, students might write a traditional essay or produce and submit a video that meets the same content requirements.

UDL also helps keep online learners engaged and motivated—two areas crucial to online student retention. Online students who stop participating cite disengagement with the material as a primary reason, second only to time-management issues (Willging & Johnson, 2009). In universal design, online courses are "salted" throughout with messages and content that ties current activities back to prior learning and forward to terminal course objectives. By showing learners why they are performing course tasks, UDL-rich online courses guide all students to be more involved in constructing their own learning.

And, of course, UDL benefits learners with disabilities, who, when they are permitted to select their own paths through the course materials, are better able to experience the content, demonstrate their knowledge, and stay on task.

Back to our two profs

So, what about Carrie Oakey and Gene Poole? The videos of music performances in Oakey's Art of Listening course couldn't be transcribed into text. The aim of UDL is not to create a text version of all multimedia but to offer multiple paths to the content where it's possible. Because the audio is the key component of each performance, and because Oakey's goal is for students to develop a critical ear, the very definition of her course precludes full participation by a learner with a hearing disability.

In this case, Oakey isn't required to create an accommodation at the level of her course. However, if a hearing-disabled learner wanted to fulfill an arts course requirement, there should at least be another course that they could take.

Oakey's assignment (write a two-page response paper), though, could be expanded using UDL principles. Perhaps students could write the two-page paper or record a three-minute audio or video response. Again, as long as the alternatives share common requirements and objectives, having the choice benefits all learners.

Poole's PowerPoint-to-video conversions for Cell Biology required a significant amount of effort on his part and on the part of the staffers who assisted with the conversion. However, it's a one-time cost. Poole can share the shorter media items semester after semester; when content or methods change, he will need to rerecord only a short item, not the entire hour of content.

Poole's students benefit too because they can consume the videos in small bursts, which helps with motivation and engagement. In fact, to provide multiple reinforcements for his students, Poole might wish to ask students to view only the first few videos and then come back into the online course to practice in a simulation, take a quiz, or respond in a discussion.

The payoff for both professors is that using UDL principles in their online classes allows them to move away from merely presenting information and toward allowing learners to choose their own way to move through the material; demonstrate their skills; and engage with the content, with one another, and with the prof.

Epilogue

On the 56 bus, a student in Cell Biology is watching a video snippet on her smartphone. Her commute to work used to be time for catching up on Facebook, but now she has 30 minutes twice per day when she can study for class. Being able to "go to class" during her commute means that she has more time at home for her family.

In a pub near the university, several graduate students in The Art of Listening are gathering to record their video response to the Bach concerto that Carrie Oakey shared with the students. It's a version of the same concerto—with one of these students playing the role of on-camera reporter and the remaining students performing the piece as they have transcribed it for a rock-and-roll band.

In a town 130 miles from the university, a student in Cell Biology rolls his wheelchair over to his computer and logs into the course. He watches a few of Gene Pool's videos, takes a self-review quiz, and posts his ideas about the upcoming research project into a class discussion forum—just like everybody else in the class.

References

Center for Applied Special Technology [CAST]. (2013). *UDL guidelines.* www.cast.org/library/UDLguidelines

Smith, A., Rainie, L., & Zickuhr, K. (2011, July 19). College students and technology. https://www.pewresearch.org/internet/2011/07/19/college-students-and-technology

Willging, P., & Johnson, S. (2009, October). Factors that influence students' decision to drop out of online courses. *Journal of Asynchronous Learning Networks, 13*(9), 115–127. http://sloanconsortium.org/sites/default/files/v13n3_10willging_0.pdf

Culturally Responsive Teaching and UDL

Gwen Bass and Michael Lawrence-Riddell

Creating educational experiences for our students that integrate universal design for learning (UDL) and culturally responsive teaching (CRT), a philosophy of education that centers students' cultural backgrounds as essential to their learning (Ladson-Billings, 1994), is a powerful tool for preparing them for today's professional environment, which increasingly acknowledges diversity as integral to success. As Chita-Tegmark et al. (2012) writes, "If both the increasingly global society made possible by modern technology and the culturally diverse societies in which we live are considered, success in the twenty-first century requires individuals to incorporate more than a single culture's system of thought" (p. 18).

The students in our classrooms arrive with a diverse set of learning needs and a range of cultural experiences and identities. Learning, along with the ways a person's brain changes in response to new experiences, must be looked at within the context and the culture in which they occur (Chita-Tegmark, 2012). People from different cultures arrive in our classrooms with culturally based differences that influence how they interact with our courses. This does not mean that certain students (with certain identities) are capable of doing higher level work while other students (with other identities) are not. In other words, UDL and CRT are not about de facto tracking. Rather, by incorporating a range of learning strategies to address multiple perspectives, values, entry points, and opportunities for acquiring and demonstrating knowledge, educators can amplify the benefits of diversity.

While educators need not be experts on every culture, they should make efforts to ensure that their students' experience their own learning styles and their own cultures in the teaching and learning process. One way that I have given students the opportunity to understand their own identities and to feel that they are honored in the class is through "identity mapping." I have adapted this activity from a Facing History, Facing Ourselves lesson (https://www.facinghistory.org/resource-library/teaching-strategies/identity-charts). Here, students create identity maps at the beginning of a course, and when they are finished with them, we display them on the wall of the classroom—a visual reminder of the diversity of cultures, opinions, experiences, interests, and passions that make up our classroom community. Something I view as core to my job as an educator is to encourage students to see the world, and every situation, from various perspectives. This must be represented in the curriculum and used to teach students to explore issues from multiple angles and value collaboration across lines of difference so they can ask important questions about power dynamics and voice.

If we are being proactive and predictive about the diversity of learning styles and skills that UDL encourages us to consider, we should also strive to incorporate this same kind of prediction and proaction as it relates to cultural diversity in our classrooms. If we design our instruction in such a way that centers students' diversity as a core strength to be amplified, we will have a greater chance of being successful. Thinking about multiple means of representation, expression, and engagement when designing this kind of course material is essential. In the same way that you might consider creating coursework that anticipates the needs of all of the diverse types of learners in your room, examine how your coursework relates to, represents, and honors the cultural diversity within the students you teach. By using this as an overarching framework, you can ask yourself, "In what ways am I providing entry and connections into my coursework that speak to the diverse experiences of my learners?"

We need to ensure that in cultivating real-world connections and experiences for our students, we are addressing all learners. Similarly, educators must also include viewpoints and narratives that have not been part of "traditional" course materials. The Center for Advanced Research on Language Acquisition at the University of Minnesota (n.d.) has defined culture as "shared patterns of behaviors and interactions, cognitive constructs, and affective understanding that are learned through a process of socialization. These shared patterns identify the members of a culture group while also distinguishing those of another group." Applying UDL and CRT is a powerful shift in making our classrooms a space for all learners—individual students have more of an opportunity to see themselves reflected in the work they are being asked to do, which in turn creates a more inclusive community and helps model the professional world our students will soon enter.

Simply providing choice for students in terms of the input of information or their own output is a step toward a culturally responsive classroom, as is inherent in the guiding principles of UDL—providing multiple means of representation, expression, and engagement. By honoring the fact that there are multiple ways to communicate ideas, you provide entry points for students from a multitude of backgrounds. As Chita-Tegmark et al. (2012) argue, "People from different cultures may learn the same things, but they may learn them differently" (p. 18). We need to be prepared for that reality, and we need to proactively create learning experiences that recognize and honor cultural differences.

References

Center for Advanced Research on Language Acquisition, University of Minnesota. (n.d.). What is culture? http://www.carla.umn.edu/culture/definitions.html

Chita-Tegmark, M., Gravel, J. W., Serpa, M. L. B., Domings, Y., & Rose, D. H. (2012). Using the universal design for learning framework to support culturally diverse learners. *Journal of Education, 192*(1), 17–22.

Ladson-Billings, G. (1994). What we can learn from multicultural education research. *Educational Leadership, 51*(8), 22–26.

Further reading

Degner, J. (2016, November 15). How universal design for learning creates culturally accessible classrooms. *Education Week.* https://www.edweek.org/tm/articles/2016/11/14/udl-creates-cultural-competency-in-classroom.html

Hammond, Z. (2014). *Culturally responsive teaching and the brain: Promoting authentic engagement and rigor among culturally and linguistically diverse students.* Corwin Press.

James, K. (2018). Universal design for learning (UDL) as a structure for culturally responsive practice. *Northwest Journal of Teacher Education, 13*(1). https://doi.org/10.15760/nwjte.2018.13.1.4

Kieran, L., & Anderson, C. (2018). Connecting universal design for learning with culturally responsive teaching. *Education and Urban Society, 51*(9), 1202–1216. https://doi.org/10.1177/0013124518785012

Rao, K. (2015). Universal design for learning and multimedia technology: Supporting culturally and linguistically diverse students. *Journal of Educational Multimedia and Hypermedia, 24*(2), 121–137.

Implementing Accessible Course Policies

Paige Hoffman and Amanda Hurlbut

Access can mean many different things in a classroom. For students with disabilities, access means having material, spaces, and coursework accessible for a variety of learning needs. Access can also mean recognizing the limits of time, money, and basic necessities when students come from a range of socioeconomic backgrounds. Of course, we also have universal access in education, which states that all people have equal opportunity in education, regardless of marginalized positions and social inequities (Dolmage, 2015).

At its heart, access is about recognizing the differences in students' lived experiences and designing and teaching courses that work with these differences. How then can we make classrooms accessible for a diverse student population with a wide range of learning needs?

Here we outline three simple techniques for increasing accessibility.

1. **Have more assignments worth less**. We all understand that the lives of teachers are packed full with obligations and responsibilities. Having more assignments means grading more assignments, but courses with a lot of low-stakes assignments help students in a number of ways. First, taking this approach means that students will not bomb the course because they got one bad grade. For students who have health issues, kids, or elderly parents; work multiple jobs; or struggle to find food to nourish their bodies enough to learn, this approach recognizes these factors. Second, it provides students with more feedback from instructors to facilitate deeper learning. Rather than having one big project due during midterms and another due toward the end of the course, students work on assignments throughout the course with opportunities to demonstrate growth and improvement from start to finish.

2. **Be strategic and fair when offering extra credit.** Extra credit continues to be a controversial policy in college courses (Osborn, 2011). Although extra credit is something students crave and can be effective when done strategically, many teachers offer extra credit opportunities at the last minute, such as when special events or speakers are hosted on campus. This can be an inaccessible opportunity for some. Was there enough warning so that students who are deaf or hard of hearing could request an interpreter or other accommodation services, such as communication access real-time translation (CART)? What about students who have family or childcare obligations or both? Does the event conflict with a student's job responsibilities? Are there other conflicts that prevent students from being able to attend and therefore earn some extra credit?

To offer equitable extra credit opportunities, faculty must provide ample notice of the event so that students can request accommodations or make arrangements that enable them to attend. Another option is to offer choice. For students who cannot attend a live event, consider allowing them to demonstrate their participation in a live-streamed event. Or provide an alternative by allowing students to complete extra credit work at home. Many libraries offer students access to video-streaming services, such as Kanopy, that can be accessed from anywhere.

3. **Assess skills differently.** A heavy reliance of multiple choice and true-false questions as assessments of learning certainly makes grading easier, but designing all assessments in this way does a disservice to the many students who struggle to present their understanding of the material in response to objective exam questions. Create assignments that allow students to rehash, learn, and assess in different ways. Utilize short answers, essays, and projects that highlight their ability to explain and build on concepts. If you already have lots of assignments worth a lesser percentage, why not test this knowledge in different and more equitable ways? People learn differently and apply knowledge in diverse ways. Let students grapple with course content beyond the standard multiple choice and true-false exams. Assess knowledge and skills in ways that foster creativity and a fuller understanding of course content.

Hopefully you'll find these tips useful as you work to implement more accessible policies in your courses. There are many more resources you can use to make your classes accessible. Working toward universal design for learning principles and practices that recognize differences and social inequalities is a must in today's classrooms.

References

Dolmage, J. (2015). Universal design: Places to start. *Disability Studies Quarterly, 35*(2). https://doi.org/10.18061/dsq.v35i2.4632

Hamilton, L., & Armstrong, E. (2012, July 2). Social life and social inequality. *The Chronicle of Higher Education*. https://www.chronicle.com/article/Social-LifeSocial/132631

Osborn, C. (2011, June 16). Should you offer extra credit? *The Chronicle of Higher Education*. https://www.chronicle.com/blogs/onhiring/should-you-offer-extra-credit/29055

Designing for Accessibility: How to Front-Load Your Course with UDL Principles

Caran Howard

Accessibility is a big deal. We include statements about accessibility in our syllabi and on our institutional websites. We also need to ensure that we comply with the Rehabilitation Act of 1973, the Americans with Disabilities Act of 1990 (ADA), the Americans with Disabilities Act Amendments Act of 2008 (ADAAA), and Section 508 of the Rehabilitation Act, as amended in 1998, and that learners with disabilities have "equal access" to online course content.

And yet every semester, accessibility and IT offices find themselves overloaded with requests for closed captioning or transcripts and for online material accommodations for students with disabilities. Students fail tests and miss assignment deadlines because important infographics or images do not have alternative tag descriptions, because YouTube videos—crucial to the first exam—have no closed captioning, or because they need to read 20 scanned and untagged PDFs that a screen reader just cannot read.

With tools like Ally Accessibility Checker embedded in learning management systems and the availability of screen readers, learners of all abilities have more options for accessing their content. With Ally, students can download their syllabus or PowerPoints as audio files and listen as they commute. They can also use braille readers to take quizzes.

Having more options for accessing content is great as long as the content we are creating is great. Unless we create and collect content that meets accessibility standards, students do not have equal access to content.

However, when we create and collect digital content that follows universal design for learning (UDL) principles for multiple means of representation, specifically for perception or accessibility, then our online courses are already accessible to a majority of learners with diverse abilities.

When we create or collect content using UDL principles, our goal is to have online or blended courses that look ahead and meet learners' needs before they even enroll in the course, and before we get an accommodation letter from the student accessibility office. We may not have to scramble to make accommodations before something is due. Designing for accessibility means anticipating needs based on trends and institutional data, and creating a course where content is accessible to the greatest number of diverse students.

Is front-loaded accessibility a lot of work? Yes, but it is front-loaded work. This means it is done in advance and with intent-filled course design, careful content authoring and editing, and commitment to teaching all students.

Follow these steps to create content that is accessible to all students:

- Run the accessibility checker as you create Word Docs (https://webaim.org/techniques/word), PDFs (https://webaim.org/techniques/acrobat), and PowerPoints (https://webaim.org/techniques/powerpoint) and correct the errors and warnings as you work.
- Use the heading and list functions in Word and use an accessible font, such as Verdana.
- Use high-contrast colors and avoid using underlining and bold to make a point.
- Provide links to online resources and/or order a digital course packet for hard-to-come-by resources instead of scanning and uploading as documents as PDFs.
- Include only necessary and content-driven images and add alternative text descriptions as you work.
- Use captioning when you record lecturettes and edit for accuracy. You can record with captioning and edit closed captioning in your Panopto and Zoom. You can also edit captioning in recordings you upload into YouTube.

Follow these steps to assess digital content you collect for accessibility:

- Test that PDFs you find online are tagged and searchable.
- Ask publishers to provide online or digital content (such as PowerPoints) that meet accessibility standards.
- Provide links for websites with working links and accessible font and contrast colors.

- Check that third-party YouTube videos have accurate captioning. If they do not, provide a transcript or ask your accessibility office to run the video through Amara.
- Provide students with accessibility statements and contact information for online tools such as Blackboard, Zoom, VoiceThread, YouTube, Poll Everywhere, and Flipgrid.

Further reading

Bureau of Internet Accessibility. (2017, May 22). Why websites need an accessibility statement. https://www.boia.org/blog/why-websites-need-an-accessibility-statement

CAST. (2018). Universal design for learning guidelines version 2.2. http://udlguidelines.cast.org

Haynie, D. (2014, April 4). Students with disabilities meet challenges in online courses. *U.S. News and World Report*. https://www.usnews.com/education/online-education/articles/2014/04/04/tips-for-online-students-with-disabilities

University of Washington. (n.d.). Captioning your own video for free. https://www.washington.edu/accessibility/videos/free-captioning

U.S. Department of Education. (n.d.). Accessibility statement. https://www2.ed.gov/notices/accessibility/index.html

Creating Accessible Video for the Online Classroom

Krista Greear and Patrick R. Lowenthal

Videos are being integrated more and more into the online classroom. However, they can create barriers for learners with hearing problems. If a student asks for an ADA accommodation for a video, you will be scrambling at the last minute to create a text supplement. That's why it's good practice to create a text supplement at the same time that you create a video.

Many faculty use separate transcripts to add text for hearing-impaired students. But this makes it challenging for a deaf or hard-of-hearing student to absorb the visual and auditory information simultaneously as they need to shift back and forth between the images and text. The better way to create accessible video is with captions that appear within the video itself, allowing learners to read the text with the images. While captioning takes time, the steps are not difficult to master, and there are a variety of options for adding captions to online videos.

A common way to caption videos is to do it yourself, either in two steps, creating the transcript and then adding it to the video, or in one step with software that creates the captions automatically from the video. While the former process sounds more time-consuming, automated systems often make a lot of mistakes and require editing the results later on. This is why some people prefer making the transcript manually. Below is a description of each process.

Two-step process

Step one: *create the transcript*

- **Manual creation:** Type a script before you create the video and then read from it when recording your video narration. This option can work well, but it can be very challenging for faculty using video in a less scripted manner (e.g., instructional screencasts of software).

- **Desktop software:** Speak into speech-to-text software like Dragon NaturallySpeaking for PC to translate your words into written text. The quality has come a long way from the early days of speech recognition, but the results will still need to be edited for errors.

Step two: *sync the transcript to video*

- **Web-based software:** Upload your video to YouTube and then upload the transcript file afterward. The system will read the transcript and sync the two by determining when the text needs to appear on the screen.
- **Commercial provider:** You can pay a commercial provider a fee to take your video and transcript and sync the two. These providers use human or computer efforts to ensure the captions show at the appropriate time.

One-step process

Another option is to use software that creates captions right off the audio in the video, thus avoiding the two-step process outlined above. However, the features, methodology, and capabilities of each software program vary widely.

- **Web-based software:** YouTube is a popular video application that has built-in speech recognition to create automated captions. Again, the results will need to be edited for accuracy.
- **Desktop software:** Some lecture-capture or presentation-creation software have a built-in captioning feature. Captivate allows you to (a) create a presentation, create a transcript separately, and then sync the words with the video to create captions or (b) create a presentation, export audio, submit audio to a vendor for captioning with speech-to-text software to have the computer create a transcript, then sync the words with the video to create captions. Camtasia is another popular option. You can add captions manually with Camtasia or use its speech-to-text tool to create the transcript. (Please note the captioning feature is currently available only for the PC version; the Mac version of Camtasia does not have this capability.) In our experience, some faculty find using Camtasia easier than others do.

Pay for it: commercial providers

Given the time it takes to create captions yourself, many colleges and universities use commercial providers to caption videos for online course. Commercial providers can (a) create or edit a transcript only, (b) sync or merge the transcript to a video, or (c) create an interactive transcript that is searchable by word. Some providers can also translate videos and even add captions to videos that you didn't create and do not own. Rev.com is a popular option. Receive captions in 24–48 hours for as little as $1 per minute.

Pay for it: freelancers

One last option is to pay a freelancer to create a transcript for you. Fiverr.com lists dozens of freelancers who will caption 15 minutes of video for $5 (often more for multiple speakers or quick turnaround). If you have flexibility, freelancers might be the cheapest way to get a transcript created and therefore are extremely useful if you are paying for these services out of your own pocket.

Additional resources

Still looking for more support? Check out these two websites:

- **Captioning Your Own Video for Free (University of Washington):** http://www.washington.edu/accessibility/videos/free-captioning. This website covers topics including captioning your own video for free, how to add caption files to video, adding captions to YouTube videos, and adding captions to videos on web pages.
- **Caption It Yourself (Described and Captioned Media Program):** https://www.dcmp.org/ciy. This website includes sections on web-based captioning and subtitling tools, desktop captioning and subtitling software, caption-ready video hosting providers, how to caption videos yourself, and guidelines for captions.

Video captioning is not difficult and is a critical component for creating an accessible online course.

Social Media Use in Online Courses: Accessibility Considerations

Kathleen Bastedo

Last month we looked at privacy considerations and how to address them when using social media tools. This month we look at accessibility considerations. With recent accessibility lawsuits against institutions such as Penn State, Harvard, and MIT (see this link: http://www.d.umn.edu/~l-carlson/atteam/lawsuits.html), it is a good idea to address accessibility when using common social media tools such as Facebook, Twitter, LinkedIn, or YouTube in an online course.

Accessibility syllabus statement suggestions

All courses should include an accessibility statement in the syllabus. But these are often just a paragraph that provides students with minimal course accessibility information and refers students directly to the student accessibility office with issues. This is the perfect place to also mention which social media tools will be used in the course. Since each type of tool can have its own potential accessibility issues, it's best to provide students with some information on each tool that will be implemented in the course. Instructors may also invite these students to personally discuss any needs or concerns with the instructor they may have regarding the use of these tools.

Keep in mind that there may be some students who do not already have accounts for certain social media applications. Doing the following can help students, all students, be successful in the use of social media in the online environment:

1. Include the purpose of using the application in the course. Why will it be advantageous to use a communication tool outside of the LMS? What are the advantages, the goals?
2. Include guidelines as to how you expect students to use these tools, what types of usernames you recommend, and how they should submit related assignments if there are any.
3. Consider offering students the opportunity to complete an alternative project or assignment if they are not comfortable using social media.
4. Mention any cost involved if there is one.

Facebook accessibility tips

When implementing Facebook in an online course, remind students to add alternative text (a description of an image) to any image they upload to benefit users who are visually impaired. In order to make this process more automatic, though not yet perfected, back in 2016 Facebook began to implement the use of an artificial intelligence to automatically create alternative text for any image uploaded. In addition, the mobile version of Facebook has some accessibility options that may be easier to use than the browser version for some students, and so the instructor should recommend that students consider this app if they have accessibility issues.

Twitter accessibility tips

When using Twitter, it is a good idea to recommend that students add hashtags and usernames to the end of a post as this order makes it easier to follow a thread for students with low vision, learning disabilities, or for those students who use a screen reader (a software product that reads text on a computer screen for students who are blind or visually impaired). Provide students with basic information on how to tweet, what is a hashtag, what are followers, and what is the definition of a retweet. Provide a list of commonly used text shortcuts (e.g., LOL—laughing out loud) and have students keep the use of text shortcuts to a minimum to help those unfamiliar with shortcuts. In addition, recommend that students include prefixes when they are adding media, such as [PIC] for an image, [VIDEO] for a video link, or [AUDIO] for an audio file.

YouTube accessibility tips

When incorporating YouTube into the online course environment, provide specific reasons for its use. Will students be expected to create their own videos? If so, recommend that they create transcripts before creating the video. This ensures that important points are covered. The transcript will also make it easier to add updates and edits; it will have a more professional appearance (fewer *ums*); and it will also make it easier for students to add captions, which would be beneficial for a student with a hearing impairment, an ESOL student, or a student with a learning disability (Burgstahler, 2017). Also suggest that students who need captioning view this video on how they can search for captioned YouTube videos: https://youtu.be/d1sRvT2xFL0.

Keep in mind that some accessibility issues remain inherent in each tool generally due to the fact that these tools are constantly changing and evolving. Although accessibility concerns remain, each social media tool mentioned here continues to improve accessibility features for all of their users and many of the tools encourage user feedback as problems arise.

Take a look at this list of resources for ensuring that your courses are accessible to all students: https://bit.ly/2IzCEMf.

Reference

Burgstahler, S. (2017). Real connections: Making distance learning accessible to everyone. http://www.washington.edu/doit/real-connections-making-distance-learning-accessible-everyone

About the Contributors

Kenneth L. Alford, PhD, is a professor of church history and doctrine at Brigham Young University. After serving almost 30 years on active duty in the United States Army, he retired as a colonel in 2008. While on active military duty, Alford served in numerous assignments, including the Pentagon, eight years teaching computer science at the United States Military Academy at West Point, and four years as a department chair and professor teaching strategic leadership at the National Defense University in Washington, DC. He has published and presented on a wide variety of topics during his career.

Bridget Arend, PhD, is the owner of Intentional College Teaching and is affiliate faculty and the former executive director of the Office of Teaching and Learning at the University of Denver.

Gwen Bass, PhD, spent nearly 10 years in pre-K–12 schools as an early childhood educator, special education teacher, and school counselor, and she currently directs the Teacher Leadership division of Professional and Graduate Education at Mount Holyoke College. Bass frequently presents on inclusive classroom practices, behavior management, child development, child welfare systems, parent education, measurement and evaluation of social emotional skills in schools, and trauma-sensitive teaching. She uses her research and expertise to enhance opportunities for marginalized students and improve educational access and outcomes for children with learning differences. Additionally, Bass provides educational and parenting consultation and training for caregivers, teachers, and social workers.

Kathleen Bastedo, MEd, has been an instructional designer at the University of Central Florida since 2006. She assists faculty with the design, development, and delivery of online courses. Her area of specialization involves universal design for learning and the accessibility of digital course materials. Her online research interests include accessibility of online course materials for individuals with disabilities, simulations and training (VR and AR), and the learning sciences. Bastedo earned a master's degree in curriculum and instruction from the University of South Florida and a bachelor of science degree in occupational therapy from Utica College of Syracuse University.

Bradley Bowers, PhD, is a professor of English at Barry University in Miami Shores, Florida. He teaches American literature and 20-century British and world literatures. Bowers holds a PhD in English from the University of North Carolina at Chapel Hill. He has been a visiting scholar at Columbia University in New York, the American Academy in Rome, and American University of Rome. He has published on such topics as British and American modernism, Italian futurism, Ernest Hemingway, and Virginia Woolf and edited an essay collection titled The Da Vinci Code in the Academy.

Deborah Bracke, PhD, is an associate professor of education at Augustana College. Her professional career is marked by a variety of wonderful teaching and learning experiences. She taught special education for eight years and immediately recognized the value of differentiated instruction and classroom community. After receiving her PhD from the University of Iowa, she began teaching at Augustana College. Her signature course, Methods of Inclusion, is required for all education majors. In addition to teaching, Dr. Bracke has served as the chair of the Faculty Welfare Committee and chair of the Business and Education Division. She is the faculty advisor for Augustana's men's and women's tennis teams and accompanies teacher candidates annually to the Florida School for the Deaf and Blind for an annual one-week immersion experience.

Rebecca Brent, EdD, is the president of Education Designs Inc., a consulting firm in Cary, North Carolina. She has more than 35 years of experience in education and specializes in staff development in engineering and the sciences, teacher preparation, and evaluation of educational programs at both precollege and college levels. She holds a certificate in evaluation practice from the Evaluators' Institute at George Washington University. She has authored or coauthored roughly 65 papers on effective teaching and faculty and teaching staff development. Prior to entering private consulting, she was an associate professor of education at East Carolina University, where she won an outstanding teacher award. In 2014, she was named a fellow of the American Society for Engineering Education. Brent also codirected the American Society for Engineering Education National Effective Teaching Institute from 1995 to 2015 and coauthored *Teaching and Learning STEM: A Practical Guide* (Jossey-Bass, 2016). Follow Brent on Twitter @RebeccaBrent.

Andrew J. Cano is a virtual learning librarian and assistant professor at the University of Nebraska–Lincoln.

Robin E. Clark, JD, is a clinical assistant professor of business law at West Texas A&M University. She joined the Paul and Virginia Engler College of Business in 2013. She received a BBA in general business from West Texas State University in 1983 and a JD with honors from the University of Texas in 1990. Clark was admitted to the State Bar of Texas in 1990. Since graduating from law school, Dr. Clark has practiced transactional law in Amarillo.

Ed Cunliff, PhD, is a professor of adult and higher education in the College of Education and Professional Studies at the University of Central Oklahoma. His prime goal is to help learners achieve their goals, and he does that through teaching and facilitating learning. His areas of teaching and research interests include adult learners, applied research, transformative learning, managing adult education programs, and the organization and administration of higher education. Cunliff received his PhD in adult and community education in 1983 and his MA in human relations, with an emphasis on counseling and organizational development, in 1974—both from Oklahoma University. He graduated with a BS in Spanish from DePauw University in 1969 and also attended the University of Madrid, Spain, in 1968.

Flower Darby is passionate about increasing student success through engaging, innovative teaching approaches and effective instructional design. As a faculty member and director of teaching for student success at Northern Arizona University, Darby designs in-person, online, and blended classes that support students in their learning. She has taught at NAU for more than 24 years in a range of areas, from English literature to educational technology to dance to Pilates. She loves to apply effective teaching and learning principles across the disciplines both in her classes and in those of the faculty she supports at NAU. Darby is the author, with James M. Lang, of *Small Teaching Online* (Jossey-Bass, 2019).

Karen Dunlap, EdD, is a professor of teacher education at Texas Woman's University. Her research and writing focus on the development of 21st-century teacher leaders, integration of instructional practice and appropriate pedagogically sound web-based tools, and preservice to experienced teacher identity development. An author of multiple book chapters and journal articles, Dunlap served Texas public school students for more than 25 years in a variety of teacher, administrative, and supervisory positions before becoming a faculty member at TWU.

Emily Faulconer, PhD, is the research associate in the Department of STEM Education for the College of Arts and Sciences, Worldwide Campus, at Embry-Riddle Aeronautical University. She provides service to her professional community as a member of the Journal of College Science Teaching advisory board and an online advisor for the National Science Teachers Association. Her research agenda centers on best practices in online education.

Ginger R. Fisher, PhD, is an associate professor of biology and director of the Master's in Biomedical Science program at the University of Northern Colorado. She conducts research in biology education and teaches a wide range of courses from introductory biology to graduate level courses in physiological ecology.

Joan Flaherty, MA, MSc, is an associate professor in the School of Hospitality, Food and Tourism Management at the University of Guelph, where she teaches communications. She is also the author of *The Counterintuitive Writer: A Writing Guide for Students . . . and for Others* (Rock's Mills Press, 2018).

Tammy Garren, PhD, is a contract learning designer. She recently joined Strategic Education Inc., where she serves as the senior learning designer. She has been teaching in higher education, both online and face-to-face, for over a decade. Garren holds a PhD in educational theory and practice with an emphasis in instructional technology from the University at Albany. She also holds a combined BA/MA in American History from the University at Albany.

Krista Greear is an access text and technology program manager at the University of Washington. Specifically, she provides accessible textbooks, course packs, articles, and other instructional materials. She has served in higher education disability services, providing students with alternate text since 2007. She was involved with the UW's Web Council, the Approaches on Accessibility interest group, the Online Advising group, Husky Toastmasters, and WAPED.

Paul Hanstedt, PhD, is the founding director of the Center for Academic Resources and Pedagogical Excellence (CARPE) at Washington and Lee University. He has helped dozens of colleges and universities in the US and Asia with general education and pedagogical reform and is the recipient of several teaching awards, including a 2013 State Council for Higher Education in Virginia Outstanding Faculty Award and the 2014 CASE-Carnegie Virginia Professor of the Year Award. He has authored several books, including *General Education Essentials: A Guide for College Faculty* and, most recently, *Creating Wicked Students: Designing Courses for a Complex World*, published by Stylus. Follow him on Twitter @CurricularGeek.

Angela Heath, PhD, teaches online computer courses at Baptist Health Systems in San Antonio, Texas.

Paige Hoffmann is a doctoral student in the Department of Multicultural Women's and Gender Studies at Texas Woman's University. She holds a master's in gender and women's studies from the University of Wisconsin–Madison. Her research interests include disability and chronic illness personal narratives and ethnographies; queer studies focusing on marginalization of asexuality in queer and disabled communities; accessible and feminist pedagogies and disability; and the intersections of race, gender and LGBTQ+ in higher education.

Caran Howard, PhD, is an instructional development specialist at the University of Northern Iowa (UNI). In 2015, she earned a PhD in social foundations of education, with an emphasis in the history of education, from the University of Iowa. Howard has more than 19 years of teaching experience in higher education and community organizations: UNI, the University of Iowa, Wartburg College, Hawkeye Community College, and the Hearst Center for the Arts.

Amanda Hurlbut, PhD, is an assistant professor of curriculum and instruction in the Teacher Education Department at Texas Woman's University. She has served in public education for over 15 years as an elementary teacher, instructional specialist, campus administrator, and teacher educator. She received her MEd in educational leadership from Dallas Baptist University and her PhD in curriculum and instruction from the University of North Texas.

Hillary Kaplowitz, PhD, is the senior instructional designer for faculty development at California State University, Northridge (CSUN). She leads campus efforts to meet the needs of faculty using technology in their teaching and collaborates on programming focused on evidence-based engaging teaching practices. In addition, she has concurrently served as a faculty lecturer at CSUN. Prior to coming to CSUN, Hillary spent 14 years producing multimedia medical education for Zephyr Medical Enterprises. Hillary holds a PhD in instructional design and technology from the Darden College of Education & Professional Studies at Old Dominion University.

Susan M. Keenan, PhD, is a professor of biology and director of the STEM Inclusive Excellence Collective at the University of Northern Colorado.

Susan Ko, PhD, is a faculty development consultant in the Office of Online Education and a clinical professor in the Department of History at the City University of New York's Lehman College. She is the author of *Teaching Online: A Practical Guide* (now in its fourth edition from Routledge) and is coauthor of the recent book *Best Practices in Designing Courses with Open Educational Resources.* Dr. Ko has more than 20 years of online teaching and faculty development experience.

Sami Lange, MLIS, is an outreach and exhibits librarian at Santa Rosa Junior College (SRJC) Libraries. She coordinates the Mahoney Library Gallery, manages the SRJC Library outreach program, and teaches Introduction to Information Literacy. She has published over 15 articles, including features in *Library Journal, Info Career Trends, Online Classroom,* and Marketing Library Services. She was awarded the SRJC Randolph Newman Faculty Award in 2014 and the SRJC Excellence in Education Award in 2016.

Michael Lawrence-Riddell serves as an executive director at The Self-Evident Media and a fellow in Entrepreneurship in Education at Mount Holyoke College. He has been an educator in one way, shape, or form for the better part of the past three decades. He has taught high school in Brooklyn, elementary school in Boston, and middle school in Amherst. While at Wesleyan University, Michael majored in African American studies and was actively involved in anti-racist activism on campus. It is when Michael is able to marry his passions for learning, history, social justice, and a better future that he is his most fulfilled. Michael brings these passions to his current work creating a multimedia, digital curriculum that looks at the histories and legacies of institutional racism. Through this work he hopes to shift the ways that we use our honest understandings of the past to shape our understandings of the present and the future.

Patrick R. Lowenthal, PhD, is an associate professor and co-coordinator of EdD in the Department of Educational Technology at Boise State University.

Wren A. Mills, PhD, is a pedagogical assistant professor teaching in the Organizational Leadership and Adult Education programs in the Educational Administration, Leadership, and Research Department at Western Kentucky University (WKU). She previously served as the assistant director for the Center for Innovative Teaching and Learning, where she prepared graduate students for their first teaching assignments and worked with faculty to integrate technology into their pedagogy. She also taught English for both WKU (21 years) and the Kentucky Community and Technical College System (14 years).

Nicki Monahan, MEd, is a facilitator in the Teaching and Learning Exchange (TLX) at George Brown College in Toronto. She works directly with faculty, providing training, support, consultation, and coaching to help advance the college's strategic goal of "excellence in teaching and learning." In her teaching practice and in her work with faculty, Monahan embraces collaboration in creating positive learning environments and is committed to inclusive practice. Monahan is a certified Personal and Professional Coach through Concordia University.

Wally Nolan is a senior instructional designer at Northern Arizona University.

Lolita Paff, PhD, serves as the associate professor of business and economics at Penn State Berks. She is an innovative teacher with expertise in flipped instruction, blended course design, teaching with technology, interaction, and engagement. Her teaching experience includes face-to-face, hybrid/blended, and online formats. In 2014, she received the MERLOT Classics Award in Business, a peer-reviewed national honor, for authoring an exemplary online learning resource. She serves on the boards of national teaching and learning organizations; leads faculty development workshops; and has been recognized for excellence in teaching, advising, and service.

Nancy Schorschinsky teaches math and chemistry at Penn State, Schuylkill.

Perry Shaw, EdD, is a professor of education at Arab Baptist Theological Seminary (ABTS), Lebanon. He also serves as a curriculum and faculty development consultant for theological schools across the globe and is active in the missional theological education movement within the International Council for Evangelical Theological Education. Shaw's passion is to help ABTS and other theological schools to develop and implement multidimensional, purpose-driven curricula that promote the development of missional leadership. Shaw also serves on the peer-review committee of the Christian Education Journal, the MTh/EdD/PhD in Education Programmes Committee for the Asia Graduate School of Theology (AGST Alliance), and the Theological Education Programme Board for the London School of Theology.

Jim Sibley is director of the Centre for Instructional Support at the Faculty of Applied Science at the University of British Columbia (UBC). Sibley has 35 years of experience in faculty development, support, and training at UBC. Sibley has served on the editorial board of the *Journal on Excellence in College Teaching* (term 2014–2017) and as an invited reviewer for the *Teaching and Learning Inquiry Journal.* He is the author of *Getting Started with Team-Based Learning* (Stylus). He is an international TBL consultant, having worked at schools in Australia, Canada, Korea, Lebanon, Pakistan, Uruguay, and the United States.

Jeanne M. Slattery, PhD, is a professor of psychology at Clarion University of Pennsylvania and has written three books on becoming an empathic, effective, and culturally aware therapist. She has been involved with Project Syllabus, a compendium of excellent syllabi in psychology, for over 20 years.

Anthony R. Sweat, PhD, is associate professor of church history and doctrine at Brigham Young University and teaches large-section, general education classes to roughly 3,000 students per year. He received his PhD in curriculum and instruction from Utah State University and centered his research on student- and teacher-level factors that influence religious education pedagogy.

Thomas J. Tobin, PhD, MSLS, PMP, MOT, CPACC, is the program area director for distance teaching and learning on the Learning Design,

Development, & Innovation (LDDI) team at the University of Wisconsin–Madison as well as an internationally recognized speaker and author on quality in technology-enhanced education. His books include *Evaluating Online Teaching: Implementing Best Practices* (2015); *The Copyright Ninja: Rise of the Ninja* (2017); *Reach Everyone, Teach Everyone: Universal Design for Learning in Higher Education* (2018); and *Going Alt-Ac: A Guide to Alternative Academic Careers* (2020).

Maryellen Weimer, PhD, has served as editor of *The Teaching Professor* since the newsletter began in 1987. Her *Learner-Centered Teaching: Five Key Changes to Practice* (2nd ed.) (Jossey-Bass, 2013) remains one of the most influential books for educators looking to adopt a learner-centered approach in their classrooms. Dr. Weimer's other books include *Inspired College Teaching: A Career-Long Resource for Professional Growth* (Jossey-Bass, 2010), *Enhancing Scholarly Work on Teaching and Learning Professional Literature that Makes a Difference* (Jossey-Bass, 2006), and *Improving Your Classroom Teaching* (Sage Publications, 1993). Dr. Weimer is a professor emerita of teaching and learning at Penn State Berks and won Penn State's Milton S. Eisenhower Award for distinguished teaching in 2005. Weimer has consulted with more than 600 colleges and universities on instructional issues and regularly keynotes national meetings and regional conferences. You can reach Dr. Weimer at grg@psu.edu.

Jane West, EdD, is an associate professor and director of doctoral programs for the Tift College of Education and has been a Mercer University faculty member since 2009. She teaches graduate courses in qualitative research, academic writing, and curriculum and instruction. Her teaching experience spans 30 years and includes experience in preschool, elementary school, middle school, and university settings. Her scholarly interests focus on applications of a cognitive apprenticeship framework for graduate students' learning, particularly in doctoral education. Her research has also included work in the areas of children's literature and response-based pedagogies, the social aspects of literacy learning, and raising the quality of elementary teachers' writing.

Beverly Wood, PhD, is the associate department chair for STEM Education at Embry-Riddle Aeronautical University's Worldwide Campus. She also teaches a wide range of mathematics and statistics courses in various delivery formats. Her research and professional development interests include the incorporation of active learning strategies in online mathematics and statistics courses.

Eric J. Yager, PhD, is an associate professor of microbiology at the Albany College of Pharmacy and Health Sciences. He holds a PhD in biomedical sciences and is a subject matter expert in the fields of immunology, microbiology, and virology. He teaches several didactic and lab-based courses to students majoring in prepharmacy, microbiology, public health, and pharmaceutical sciences. Dr. Yager is a convert to constructivism and aims to employ approaches and technologies that provide students opportunities to develop as active and independent learners.

Jillian R. Yarbrough, PhD, is a clinical assistant and the Virginia Engler Professor of Business Management at West Texas A&M University. With more than 20 years of experience in distance learning and professional technology training, she has developed a unique training style that combines academic discussion in an entertaining and dynamic team forum. Yarbrough earned a PhD, an MBA, and an MS from Texas A&M University and a BS from Texas Christian University. Yarbrough's interests include social psychology and employees, strategic alignment between employees and organizational goals, creative compensation, corporate training and development, and human relations.

Rebecca Zambrano, MA, is the director of online faculty development at Edgewood College in Madison, Wisconsin. She currently designs professional development for faculty in all content areas, mentors faculty colleagues, and helps guide the direction of college-wide faculty development efforts. Zambrano is an expert in online learning leadership, instructional design, adult learning, professional development webinar facilitation, and student motivation. Zambrano received her MA in education from the San Francisco State University and a graduate certificate in e-learning from the University of Wisconsin–Stout.

Olena Zhadko, PhD, is the director of online education at the City University of New York's Lehman College in City University of New York (CUNY). She has nearly 15 years of experience in the field of educational technology, and in advancing teaching and learning with technology. She has successfully worked at three academic centers by providing leadership and assistance in articulating and implementing effective teaching, and infusing best practices into curriculum development, delivery, and assessment through the effective use of technology. In her current role, she acts as Lehman College's senior administrator charged with the oversight of all facets of online instruction.

Additional Resources

Additional Resources from Magna Publications

BULK PURCHASES

To purchase multiple print copies of this book, please contact Magna Sales at sales@magnapubs.com or call 800-433-0499 ext. 183.

MEMBERSHIPS/SUBSCRIPTIONS

Faculty Focus
www.facultyfocus.com
A free e-newsletter on effective teaching strategies for the college classroom.

The Teaching Professor Membership
www.TeachingProfessor.com
The Teaching Professor is an annual membership that reflects the changing needs of today's college faculty and the students they teach. This new fully online version of the newsletter that faculty have enjoyed for more than 30 years includes the best of the print version—great articles and practical, evidence-based insights—but also many new features including video, graphics, and links that make it an even more indispensable resource.

Academic Leader Membership
www.Academic-Leader.com
Academic Leader covers the trends, challenges, and best practices today's academic decision-makers. Members gain access to the latest thinking in academic leadership and learn how peers at other
institutions are solving problems, managing change, and setting direction. New articles are published throughout the month.

CONFERENCES

The Teaching Professor Conference
www.TeachingProfessorConference.com
This event provides an opportunity to learn effective pedagogical techniques, hear from leading teaching experts, and interact with colleagues committed to teaching and learning excellence. Join more than 1,000 educators from around the country.

Attendees hear from a roster of prestigious experts and nationally recognized thought leaders. A broad mix of plenary addresses, concurrent sessions, and timely roundtable discussions leave no topic untouched.

Leadership in Higher Education Conference
www.AcademicLeadershipConference.com
The Leadership in Higher Education Conference provides higher-education leaders with an opportunity to expand leadership skills with proactive strategies, engaging networking, time-saving tips, and best practices.

BOOKS

The Academic Leader's Handbook: A Resource Collection for College Administrators
https://www.amazon.com/dp/B0764KMC5Z
The Academic Leader's Handbook: A Resource Collection for College Administrators details an array of proven management strategies and will help further your achievements as a leader in higher education. Discover new leadership tools and insights at departmental, administrative, and executive levels.

Active Learning: A Practical Guide for College Faculty
https://www.amazon.com/dp/B071ZN8R32
Learn how to apply active learning methods in both small and large classes as well as in an online teaching environment. Whether you are new to active learning methods or experienced with them, this comprehensive reference book can guide you every step of the way.

The College Teacher's Handbook: A Resource Collection for New Faculty
https://www.amazon.com/dp/0912150688
The College Teacher's Handbook: A Resource Collection for New Faculty provides the essential tools and information that any new teacher in higher education needs to confidently lead a college classroom.

Essential Teaching Principles: A Resource Collection for Adjunct Faculty
https://www.amazon.com/dp/0912150246
This book provides a wealth of both research-driven and classroom-tested best practices to help adjuncts develop the knowledge and skills required to run a successful classroom. Compact and reader-friendly, this book is conveniently organized to serve as a ready reference whenever a new teaching challenge arises—whether it's refreshing older course design, overcoming a student's objection to a grade, or fine-tuning assessments.

Essential Teaching Principles: A Resource Collection for Teachers
https://www.amazon.com/dp/0912150580
This book serves as a quick and ready reference as you encounter the challenges of teaching college-level material in the high school classroom. For an AP or IB teacher, there's no better resource.

Faculty Development: A Resource Collection for Academic Leaders
https://www.amazon.com/dp/0912150661
Discover proven tips and insights, from top academic experts, that will help you enhance faculty development programming and training on your campus.

Flipping the College Classroom: Practical Advice from Faculty
https://www.amazon.com/dp/B01N2GZ61O
This collection is a comprehensive guide to flipping no matter how much—or how little—experience you have with it. If you are just getting started, you will learn where and how to begin. If you have been at it for a while, you will find new ideas to try and solutions to common challenges. *Flipping the College Classroom: Practical Advice from Faculty* is an invaluable resource that covers all the necessary territory.

Grading Strategies for the Online College Classroom: A Collection of Articles for Faculty
https://www.amazon.com/dp/0912150564
Do your grading practices accurately reflect your online students' performance? Do your assessment and feedback methods inspire learning? Are you managing the time you spend on these things—or is the workload overwhelming? *Grading Strategies for the Online College Classroom: A Collection of Articles for Faculty* can help you master the techniques of effective online grading—while avoiding some of the more costly pitfalls.

Helping Students Learn: Resources, Tools, and Activities for College Educators
https://www.amazon.com/dp/0912150602
This workbook is a must-have guide for faculty. While the roles in the college classroom often are defined by teachers teaching and students learning, the reality is that not many students have a clear understanding of how to learn.

Managing Adjunct Faculty: A Resource Collection for Administrators
https://www.amazon.com/dp/B01N2OVK5W
Chances are your adjunct population has been built on an ad hoc basis to fill instructional needs. As a result, your institution might not have a solid management framework to support them. That's a gap you can close with guidance from *Managing Adjunct Faculty: A Resource Collection for Administrators*. This invaluable guide offers an extensive review of best practices for managing an adjunct cohort and integrating them more fully into your campus community.

Teaching Strategies for the Online College Classroom: A Collection of Faculty Articles
https://www.amazon.com/dp/0912150483
Includes online teaching strategies ranging from building a successful start of the semester, fostering productive connections, managing challenging behavior in the online classroom, and enhancing student engagement.

The New Dean's Survival Guide: Advice from an Academic Leader
https://www.amazon.com/dp/091215070X
Find numerous tools and strategies to address challenges, successes, and issues leaders face with this comprehensive survival guide with advice for deans, provosts, and managers in higher education.